Raising Healthy Children in an Alcoholic Home

Raising Healthy Children in an Alcoholic Home

BARBARA L. WOOD

CROSSROAD • NEW YORK

1992

The Crossroad Publishing Company
370 Lexington Avenue
New York, NY 10017

Printed in the United States of America

Library of Congress Cataloging-in-Publication Data

Wood, Barbara Louise, 1949–
    Raising healthy children in an alcoholic home / Barbara L. Wood.
        p.   cm.
    Includes bibliographical references and index.
    ISBN 0-8245-1205-7 (pbk.)
    1. Children of alcoholics—Mental health.   2. Alcoholics—
Family relationships.   3. Parenting.   I. Title
RJ507.A4 W66 1992   92–15532
649'.1'024—dc20   CIP

To Christopher:
Forever my happy thought.

Contents

Acknowledgments

Writing constitutes, for me, the pursuit of an altered state. The act of writing is soothing, in itself, to the soul that lusts after knowledge and self-understanding, and is compelled to find an empathic junction with other, like souls. However, I know that I also seek, in the constant, conscious effort to organize my thoughts for a reader, a transformation. I wait for those rare and precious moments when I am able to dip below the level of conscious thought and touch some unifying insight, swelling just below the surface of my awareness.

Such moments do come, and they are immensely satisfying. They do not, of course, produce the profound alterations of perception, or enhancements of character for which I secretly long. As I reflect on the most significant psychic and emotional outcomes of my last ten years of professional writing, I find that it is the love, the support, and the companionship of those who *helped* me to write that have truly changed my outlook and transformed my way of being in the world; that have moved this formerly intractable introvert to acknowledge what I suppose to be the most fundamental principle of Kohut's self-psychology: When your back is against the wall, it is the quality of your self-objects that really counts.

This time, I needed more help than ever before. I was making the transition from scholarly writing to a more popular mode, and, at the same time, racing for my life round and round the Mommy track. There are several extraordinary women and one incomparable man whom I must thank for their efforts to keep me emotionally honest, stable, reasonably responsive, and on my feet throughout the process.

First, I owe a large debt of gratitude to my agent, Sandra Dijkstra, who was willing to take a risk on a recovery title at a time when many felt that codependence was "out." Kathy Goodwin, of the Dijkstra Agency, was an invaluable source of moral support, as well as a sensitive and gifted guide as I explored an unfamiliar genre.

Heartfelt thanks are also due the busy and accomplished women who found the time, somewhere, somehow, to read and polish this manuscript.

I would never allow a piece of professional writing to leave home without the approval of Dr. Monica Callahan. She always seems to understand, immediately, what I am trying to say, and she always finds a better way to express the most complex ideas. I am grateful for her careful editing of this manuscript, and her careful handling of its slightly anxious author as well.

Dr. Mary Ann Hoffman was insightful, and loving, as always. We have graduated from "cutting up in class" to cutting up in study groups and sailboats, and I couldn't do without it.

Dr. Christine Courtois and Dr. Lynn Dworsky assisted me with the difficult material in chapters 8 and 9. I am very grateful for their time and their willingness to share their extensive knowledge of the impact of childhood trauma and abuse.

Rebecca Robinson comes closer than most people I have ever met to doing it all—and doing it all well. I am thankful for her attention to this manuscript and for the inspiration she provided as she managed to work outside the home, remain empathically attuned and responsive to her two small children, hang wallpaper, and hold on to her sense of humor. She's been more help than she knows, and when I figure out her system, I'll write another book.

My sister-in-law, Deborah Wood, was always instantly available to help me think through a thorny issue in parenting. I am grateful for her responsiveness and her expertise in early childhood development.

Nona Kuhlman provided encouragement, reassurance, and much wise counsel this year, as she does every year. It is amazing, and wonderful, to be able to feel her warmth and love across a continent.

Dr. Lorraine Wodiska, friend, colleague, collaborator, and fellow fugitive from the fashion police, continues to believe I can do anything. Her confidence in me, and her willingness to listen, and shop as necessary, kept me believing I could continue to change and grow, even as the doubts of midlife made their appearance this year.

The first people to believe I could do anything were my parents, William and Caroline Wood. I am thankful for the foundation of self-confidence they provided for me.

In the end, of course, it all comes back to my husband, Phil Ray. He gives so much. The time, and the emotional freedom to pursue creative activity would not be there, if Phil were not there for me. His instinctive sense of what it means to be a loving and sensitive guide to children has provided essential inspiration for this book. Phil, there is so much of you in everything I do.

Author's Note

The identities of the people written about in this book have been carefully disguised in accordance with professional standards of confidentiality and in keeping with their rights to privileged communication with the author.

≡ 1 ≡

Introduction

WHY AM I OKAY?

I am definitely weird in the eyes of my friends. I play in a rock band, you know. And in rock, everybody has a story. Believe me, there are good reasons why musicians drink and drug and hang in the clubs every night until they drop. I just don't know anybody that has a "normal" family. Nobody's parents are sober, or sane. Nobody's family is still together. My buddies think it's very strange that I walked away from booze and coke, and got myself a day job and that I visit my parents whenever I can. They can't believe that it makes me happy to see my parents. They can't even believe my folks are still married.

I have a story too, though. My father was a heavy-duty drinker when I was growing up. He had—well, he still has—a terrible temper, and a way of talking to you that really makes you feel like dirt. He can also be this great guy who wants to take you hunting and fishing and will play ball all afternoon if you have the day off. Sometimes I think that was the worst part of it for me. Like, which father will be there when I get home tonight? But, Dad got sober two years ago. He's been going to AA, and at least he knows now that there's something wrong with him and that he really hurt us all those years.

I can still cry sometimes when I think of what it was like when I was younger. But if I try to figure out why I'm not messing up my life big time, like all my friends are, it's not hard to see that, bad as it was, I had some big things going for me. Look, when I do cry now, or just feel really bad, I can talk to my mom. I've always been able to do that. She knows how bad things were, and she always helped me figure out how to deal with Dad. She told me from the beginning that his problem was booze, not me. I never believed I was a loser, like he said I was, because she told me different. I had somewhere to go when things got really bad. I still have that. My friends don't. They work it out with a bottle. The bottom line? Why am I okay? I know there's love out there somewhere.

Dave—Age twenty-one

Alcohol, when used compulsively, and to excess, is an extra-ordinarily destructive drug. It not only attacks and weakens every organ system in the human body, but also distorts the drinker's ability to perceive and interpret reality, so that she is largely unable to recognize or resist the deterioration of her health and the deformation of her personality.

We know now that many of the most harmful effects of alcohol addiction are rather easily transmitted to those persons who love the drinker, or who depend on her in some important way. This is why alcoholism is called a "family disease," and why families with alcoholic members so often become "dysfunctional" families. Partners of alcoholics may remain sober, yet become so desperate to rescue the drinker from blind compulsion that they neglect their other responsibilities, including self care, and begin to suffer a serious decline in their own emotional, psychological, or physical health. Some become so obsessed with control-ling and concealing their spouse's compulsive drinking that they cannot adequately care for children in the family. This preoccupation with the drinker and her disease is the phenomenon known as "codependence."A family with an alcoholic member is just a family coping with a major illness until codependence enters the picture. It becomes a dysfunctional, "alcoholic family" when the disease of alcoholism begins to dominate family life.

Children with alcoholic and codependent parents are extremely vul-nerable. They become preoccupied with the illness, just as adults do, but they do so more easily, since their view of the world is a very "self"-centered one. Children, especially younger children, believe that they are the origin of all important events. Therefore, when their parents are in pain, they assume that they are responsible for it, and that they are obliged to "fix" it. A child's need to repair ill or injured parents is made even more urgent by his powerful love for them, and his realization that his own continued well-being depends on the health and the strength of the adults who love him.

Children of alcoholics often display a fiercer devotion to the alcoholic than do codependent adults. Furthermore, their determination to free an alcoholic family from its suffering may be far more stubborn. Driven by powerful feelings of guilt and responsibility, as well as intense fear, children will take extraordinary measures to meet a troubled family's extraordinary need. Although they feel small and fearful, they will nonetheless struggle to become sufficient unto themselves, if their parents are too ill to care for them. Then they will turn to do whatever is necessary to provide nurture and comfort to their impaired caretakers. Some children of alcoholics will become family "heroes," with achievements and honors to compensate for the family's "shame." Some will become delinquent and compulsively destructive "scapegoats," if this is what is needed to distract parents from their own torment. Some children will simply withdraw into themselves as they recognize that their needs threaten the family's precarious emotional balance.

All of the methods that children employ in an effort to ease an alcoholic family's pain require them to deny some substantial portion of their own emotional reality. Children from dysfunctional alcoholic families in which both parents are too preoccupied and too exhausted to provide the children with basic physical and emotional care, learn to ignore their fears, to deny their disappointment, and to swallow their anger and despair. Some children are able to suppress all awareness of trouble in the family, and to block the perception of their longing for love, comfort, and guidance as well. Children do these things to accommodate the family's need, and also to enhance their prospects for emotional survival when they are emotionally and psychologically isolated from both parents. Those children who are able to obliterate the pain and need they feel are, for a time, less vulnerable to physical or emotional breakdown than are children who are keenly and constantly aware of their own disappointed longing.

Detachment from pain and denial of reality are effective holding actions for the child who hurts, just as they are for the alcoholic. But children from alcoholic families eventually pay the same high price their parents pay for a defensive flight from self and truth. They cannot work well, and they cannot love well. Most importantly, they cannot love themselves.

Childhood Lost

Many children from alcoholic families enter psychotherapy when they reach adulthood. They usually describe great difficulty forming and maintaining rewarding intimate relationships. Some also report that they have trouble making long-term commitments to education, or a career, and many indicate that they are struggling with compulsive problems of their own. Alcoholism, drug addiction, eating disorders, and compulsive spending are common problems. Most of the adult children who I see in psychotherapy are caught up in an "alcoholic life-style"—whether they drink or not, they are habitually, and painfully, involved with partners and activities that endanger their physical, psychological, and spiritual health.

Some adult children consciously relate their present problems to the struggles of their childhood; others do not. Almost all, however, express a sense that they are flawed and critically deficient. They feel that they have missed some pivotal experience in childhood, that they are absent some vital body of knowledge, and lacking some essential skill, or faculty, that could impart the conviction of competence and confidence they sense in others, but cannot find in themselves. Most have survived trauma and abuse that could have been expected to destroy them, and many have established careers and material life-styles that others envy, but they still feel unworthy, emotionally detached from themselves, and isolated from the experiences and satisfactions of the "normal" people around them. They are pessimistic about the prospects for acceptance from people who seem healthy and whole. Many adult children believe that they are so deeply defective that they will never be able to establish a normal family life. They feel that alcohol, drugs, and food represent the only reliable source of comfort they can ever hope to know.

In fact, most of the adult children I see in psychotherapy *have* missed something important in their childhood. For one thing, because they were so narrowly and so desperately fixed on the need to survive, and to maintain their families, they missed many of the critical peer interactions and school experiences that children use to build up a feeling of personal value, as well as self-awareness and a capacity for creative self-expression. This failure to confront and master key developmental challenges during childhood does represent a significant loss, and does lead to a sense of insufficiency and uncertainty in dealing with peers. It also makes it harder to cope with academic and vocational challenges that arise later in life.

However, the damage that ensues from loss of experience pales in comparison with that which flows from loss of love, and the absolute devastation a child feels when he loses two parents to an obsession with alcohol and alcoholism. When both parents become too ill to demonstrate the love they feel, and neither one is able to provide guidance, support, or emotional understanding, trust is destroyed and hope is vanquished. Ultimately, self-esteem fails as well, because children of alcoholic and codependent parents do not understand that their parents are ill. These children only understand that their parents are not there, and they conclude that their parents do not care to be there. They also conclude that it is their own unworthiness that has driven their parents away. It is then that feelings of deficiency set in, that a question forms in the mind, and begins to torment the heart: "If my parents can't love me, who possibly can?"

Recovery—and Prevention

Recovery aims at rebuilding self-worth and restoring a feeling of hope and faith about human relationships. In support groups, and in psychotherapy, adult survivors of alcoholic and codependent families are encouraged to acknowledge and grieve the losses of the past. When the time is right, they are helped to engage, and gradually master, the current challenges at work and in relationships that seem so daunting, and so maddeningly elusive. As adult children allow themselves to depend, just a bit, on the insight, goodwill, and emotional support that therapists and fellow survivors extend, they come to believe that other human beings can be trusted. They also begin to believe that they can be loved.

The prospect of recovery and renewed growth for adult survivors of alcoholic families is quite good today. Mental health and addictions professionals are better informed about, and better trained to help with, the problems faced by children who grow up with alcoholic and codependent parents. Still, recovery in adulthood is typically a lengthy and painful process. Reasonably enough, adult children are terrified at the prospect of emerging from the citadels of emotional isolation, denial, and self-sufficiency that they constructed at such a cost during childhood. They hope that recovery will be a largely academic enterprise, involving the mastery of various intellectual exercises and personal meditations, and that there will be lots of home study. In short, they pray that they can pull it off alone, as they have just about everything else in their lives. Most are horrified to learn that healing can only occur in the context of intimate human relationships. Many adult children of alcoholic parents spend the bulk of their time in recovery struggling to master their terror of depending on other people for emotional care and comfort. As they see it, their longing for love and care almost destroyed them when they were small, and it seems worse than foolish to let such feelings emerge once more.

Recovery is smoother and unfolds more quickly for those adult children who have had some contact, during their childhood, with a compassionate, supportive elder—someone who provided shelter from the emotional storms raging at home, who shielded them from extremes of abuse and neglect, and who helped them to an understanding of their parents' mysterious and frightening behavior. Whether such help comes from a grandparent, an aunt, or an uncle, a family friend, a therapist, or even an older and wiser sibling, it is always a powerful force for health and continued growth. Any sustained effort to provide emotional support to a child in crisis inspires in him feelings of faith about the basic goodness of the world, and strengthens his feeling of value. Someone cares. To the child, this means that he is worth caring about. Children from alcoholic families who have an opportunity to form a relationship with a healthy and helpful adult guide come to recovery with solid feelings of hope, and with far less fear, than those who were left to struggle alone.

Parents are, of course, the most powerful figures in the life of a young child. It is their love, and their guidance, that is most cherished, most curative, and most eagerly sought. Some children are unable to accept the assurances of teachers, peers, or therapists. They never feel truly lovable or valuable until they are able to secure the understanding, acceptance, and care of their parents. Things may go horribly wrong between parents and children, and families may remain divided, tormented, and angry for years on end, but children will still want to hear that their parents care and that they want to work to make things right.

Parents, on the other hand, often feel so miserable about making serious mistakes with their children that they continue to pull away from their youngsters. The parents are afraid that they can never rectify their errors, and they choose to surrender the game rather than face the possibility of a heartbreaking rejection. They find it impossible to believe that their children can forgive the past.

Even though children may be deeply hurt, and intensely angry, they do not insist, and healthy development does not require, that parents get everything right on the first, second, or third try. Children are helped, impressed, touched, and healed by parents' willingness to acknowledge mistakes, to attempt change, and to make amends when their behavior has created pain for the family. In the end, most children will forgive anything if they believe that their parents are still trying to love them, and still trying to be their parents.

What Recovering Parents—and This Book—Can Do

This book is designed to help recovering alcoholic and codependent parents to keep trying with their children—because children *can* forgive, and because they are able to heal faster and less painfully as children than they can as adults. In fact, although a family's alcoholic crisis may be extended and severe, with turmoil and anguish that run very deep, the compassion, support, and understanding of just one parent can actually prevent serious damage to a child's sense of self, and serve to strengthen and extend his feeling of self-worth.

Raising Healthy Children in an Alcoholic Home is not a general guide to child development or child care. It is, instead, a guide to understanding the life of the alcoholic family, and the impact of parental alcoholism and codependence on the developing child. It explains the ways in which family life tends to break down in the presence of alcoholism and codependence, but it also describes a strategy for reducing and repairing damage that has occurred. This strategy, which calls for parents to provide an *emotional safety net* for their recovering children, can be implemented even if the alcoholic parent continues to drink.

The concept of the emotional safety net refers to critical elements of physical and emotional security that recovering parents must provide for children to heal, and to grow. Children need basics—food, shelter, clothing, and protection from physical harm. But they also require stability from their parents and emotional honesty, and a warm, welcoming response to their pressing emotional needs. These are precisely the functions that are most likely to break down under the pressure of parental alcoholism and codependence. And so, *Raising Healthy Children in an Alcoholic Home* provides a plan that aims at helping parents to build, or rebuild, a family structure that is constant, credible, and emotionally responsive. It proposes that recovering mothers and fathers can become *therapeutic parents*, creating an atmosphere in the home that is not only healthful, but restorative to the child in pain.

What You Will Find in *Raising Healthy Children in An Alcoholic Home*—and Where You Will Find It

This book is designed to provide support and guidance for parents who are familiar with the issue of familial alcoholism and are knowledgeable about the process of recovery, as well as parents who are very new to these topics. The experienced reader may wish to skip or skim the next two chapters of this book that describe the impact of parental alcoholism on the family. Chapter 2 explains how the drinker and his partner change under the influence of chronic alcoholism, and chapter 3 describes how children in the family may be hurt by parental alcoholism and codependence.

Chapters 4 through 10 should be helpful to readers at all levels of understanding and experience. Chapter 4 provides critical details about the concepts of therapeutic parenting and the emotional safety net. Chapters 5, 6, 7, and 8 help parents to fashion the safety net. These chapters present a plan for the establishment of emotional honesty, emotional stability, emotional responsiveness, and physical security in the recovering home. Chapter 9 provides information that should help parents decide when their children need professional assessment, in addition to parental support, and Chapter 10 discusses how parents can locate professionals who are qualified to provide assistance to families that are recovering from alcoholism and codependence.

Conclusion

If you are in the early stages of your recovery from alcoholism or codependence, you have probably found that there are days, and sometimes weeks and months when you feel overwhelmed by powerful feelings of fear, vulnerability, and helplessness. It sometimes seems that this dark time will never pass. However, as your sobriety becomes stable, and easier to maintain, the apprehension and despair that have been such constant, and unwelcome companions will start to recede. You will feel the beginnings of hope and sense the possibility of true recovery, and even joy.

Whether you are struggling to control your urge to drink, or trying to relinquish some other compulsive, hurtful behavior, your decision to seek sobriety is cause for great optimism, and exhilaration. People do get better. Families do heal. Parents and children rediscover their love, and their collective strength, and begin to grow again. Anxiety, discouragement, and even periods of severe depression are a normal, and inevitable, part of the recovery process for most people. At times they will hamper your efforts to support and guide your children, but they are not a measure of your ability or inability to become a therapeutic parent. You can shepherd your children through this period of crisis and doubt in their lives. You can work with them, a little bit each day to impart the strength, courage, and wisdom they require in order to meet and master the challenge of their own recoveries. As you keep trying to sense and provide what they need, you will instill in your children an enduring conviction of their own value and you will inspire in them lasting hope about the endless possibilities for change and self-renewal in life. Then, they too, will be able to keep trying.

= 2 =

Alcoholism and the Family

An alcoholic will often continue to drink even as alcohol destroys her physical health, devastates her family life, and carries her to the brink of professional ruin. Addictions professionals have argued for years about whether such behavior can properly be termed a "disease." The controversy turns on the massive confusion and disagreement that exists concerning the cause of chronic, compulsive drinking.

Alcoholism was once viewed as a moral problem, an expression of characterological weakness. Many people (including many alcoholics and their families) still believe this. However, there are few professionals who would publicly proclaim such a view today. The moral explanation for alcoholism was discarded when physicians began to see that people of all social, economic, and moral backgrounds get into trouble with alcohol. It became increasingly clear that alcohol itself, by disorganizing thought and confounding emotion, leads to the destructive behavior that is associated with heavy drinking.

As doctors and mental health professionals discarded the notion that only weak, bad people become alcoholics, they began to look for other factors that might lead to problematic drinking. Various attempts have been made to define "the alcoholic personality," for example. Although none has been very successful, many addictions specialists do believe that there are important psychological, familial, and emotional determinants of compulsive drinking. Other clinicians and researchers in the addictions field are certain that the roots of alcoholism will be found in the drinker's physiology, or genetic makeup, and interesting and important research into this issue continues.

For now, it is probably safest, and most logical, to assume that alcoholism, like many conditions in which the ability to perceive reality and control behavior is impaired, involves some mix of genetic, physiological, and psychological factors. It is also reasonable to suppose that this mix will be somewhat different for each individual alcoholic. I am content to call alcoholism a disease because it has, in most cases, a predictable course, with predictable and deleterious effects on personality, emotion, and behavior.

The most important thing to know about alcoholism and its effects on the drinker is that it eventually causes problems in every sphere of the drinker's life. Among the principal and most frightening effects are

- *Cognitive deterioration,* with a progressive loss of contact with reality
- *Psychological deterioration,* with the habitual use of defenses that block self-awareness and displace responsibility for the drinker's problems onto other people
- *Emotional deterioration,* with a propensity toward rage and despair
- *Behavioral deterioration,* with progressive impairment of physical capacities, and a deepening reliance on abuse and exploitation as a means of releasing and reducing emotional pain
- *Spiritual deterioration,* with a loss of hope and a diminishing sense of responsibility toward other people

Alcoholism is, in most instances, a progressive disease. That is, all of these effects become more pronounced over time.

The Family Disease

Any chronic, debilitating illness suffered by one family member eventually takes its toll on the entire family system. To the extent that the patient is mortally endangered, requires extraordinary care, and is forced to relinquish his or her role and responsibilities to other family members, he and his loved ones feel heightened anxiety, increased stress, and real heartache. If your family includes an active alcoholic, you will feel all this and more.

You will feel more because an alcoholic not only has a chronic and progressive disease—she has a disease that distorts her thinking, her mood, and her behavior. When the alterations of personality that occur under the influence are extreme and violent in character, family members are not only exasperated by the compulsive drinking but are also truly terrified of it. In many cases, spouses and children are forced to organize their lives and most of their psychological and emotional resources around the possibility that the drinker will lose control and hurt or humiliate them.

You will feel more because the alcoholic also has a disease with a moral taint, and this fills her and all those close to her with deep shame. The deep-rooted, widespread, and absolutely inaccurate view of alcoholism as a grievous characterological fault also leaves many affected families feeling emotionally isolated and hopeless about the prospects for sustained recovery.

Finally, you will feel more because the alcoholic has a disease that is frequently misunderstood and misdiagnosed by medical and mental health professionals. This intensifies the frustration, loneliness, and hopelessness that a compulsive drinker and her loved ones feel.

In short, each member of an actively alcoholic family is subjected to intense emotional stress. Often, this stress reaches traumatic proportions, and becomes a chronic feature of family life. Where the alcoholism goes untreated for years on end, and no one is able to look outside the family for support and guidance, parents and children alike begin to behave like the embattled, weary veterans of violent and ceaseless civil combat they are. They abandon grand causes and higher purposes. They do not look to growth. They do not envision the fulfillment of dreams and personal ambitions. They only struggle to survive.

Denial in Alcoholic Families

The Alcoholic. For the active alcoholic in the grip of a powerful compulsion, survival means guaranteeing access to alcohol and opportunities to drink. It also means suppressing the feelings of fear, self–contempt, and despair that deepen as her disease advances. Obviously, the alcoholic employs drink as one means of altering her painful emotional reality. She also uses a powerful psychological mechanism to suppress her awareness of what she is doing and how she feels about it. She *denies* that her drinking is a problem, and that it is destroying her health and hurting her loved ones.

Alcoholic denial is not a simple matter of lying about basic facts. It is an absolute *inability to see* or know these basic facts. How can a person who has lost two jobs on account of her drinking, who has been arrested for drunk driving, and who has been confronted by her spouse on countless occasions *not know* she is an alcoholic? Denial, which is a form of *dissociation*, is a psychological mechanism that is not fully understood by mental health professionals. We do know that it is a coping process that all human beings employ to some extent when they must function in the face of intolerable pain. For example, it is very useful to the victim of a terrible accident or a violent crime to be able to minimize the seriousness of her situation and completely disconnect from her pain and fear until she has been rescued and has the emotional and physical support a human being needs in order to safely and effectively work through an intensely traumatic event.

Unfortunately, any psychological process that can be used to advantage can also be employed self-destructively. When an individual does something that initially feels very good, like drinking to excess, and this behavior eventually results in severe emotional pain, she may be moved to disconnect from her feelings of pain so that she can continue to enjoy the good feelings that come early in a drinking cycle. This strategy places her at grave risk, however. She is behaving like an injured athlete who uses a narcotic in order to compete when she is in severe pain. The pain is an important sign of damage and the need for care. The athlete who ignores it will suffer greater injury in the future, and may face permanent disability.

WILL

I met Will during my first few weeks at the public clinic where I worked just after completing graduate school. I was familiar with research reports indicating that when cocaine is freely available to laboratory animals, they ignore food and water, and ingest this intoxicating substance until they collapse and die. However, Will taught me an early and important lesson about the way in which powerful intoxicants can dominate the life of a decent, ordinary human being.

When Will first came for treatment, he was twenty-eight years old. He was married, had a six-month-old daughter, and was an associate in a well-known law firm. He was concerned about his deepening dependence on alcohol and cocaine, and worried that his wife might leave him if he continued to squander his salary on drugs. His habit had already driven the family into serious debt.

I was surprised by the fact that Will voluntarily presented himself for treatment. Most of the patients at our drug rehabilitation clinic were referred through the criminal and juvenile justice system. I was also impressed by his ability to articulate his strong feelings for his wife and child. He cried as he spoke of his love for Janice, who had been his childhood sweetheart, and when he described his daughter, who had been born after his wife suffered several miscarriages. He also gave a vivid and convincing account of the guilt and fear he felt as he considered the ways in which his drug use was threatening his health and his family.

I felt that Will was in an early stage of his disease, and reasoned that, since his ties to his family were so strong, it would be a good idea to involve his wife in the treatment from the very beginning. It would be important to educate her about Will's problem, so that she could support his recovery and begin to look at the impact of his drinking and drugging on her own life. Furthermore, if she was willing to work with Will toward a stable sobriety, this would provide him with an important incentive to remain in treatment.

The first time that Will brought Janice to a session, I asked her, as a matter of course, what feelings she had about his addiction to alcohol and cocaine. She said the same thing that so many spouses have said to me over the years—the thing that every family member feels, deep down, about their addict's behavior. Janice said, "I think that if Will really loved me the way he says he does, he would stop spending all our money on drugs and he would stay home and help me take care of our baby."

Will was unable to meet his wife's eyes during this exchange. Hands clasped between his knees, he sat hunched over, staring grimly at the floor, until I asked her to leave us alone a short while later. I asked Will how he had reacted to Janice's expressions of doubt about the strength of his love for her. I expected him to say that he felt guilty, or ashamed, or sad. I'm sure he did feel all those things, but what he actually said shocked and surprised me. I am glad that he said it, and that I believed it, for it has helped me all through my career, as I have struggled to understand, and explain to students, spouses, and children, how good people, full of genuine love for their families, can get into so much trouble with drugs. When I asked Will how he felt about his wife's feeling that he should make good on his stated commitment to her and their child, he said, "There's something really important Janice doesn't understand." This decent, tormented young man took a deep breath and looked me in the eye. "When I need to get high, I hardly remember that she and the baby exist."

This is the true meaning of psychic and physical compulsion. Addiction, untreated, becomes the center, the ultimate meaning and purpose of existence.

A comparable cycle is set in motion when the alcoholic denies her pain, and the decline of her health and her family. Her denial enables her to continue drinking, and the drinking steadily becomes heavier and more debilitating, wreaking even greater havoc in her life. Therefore the alcoholic must drink even more, and deny even more, in order to manage her pain. The destruction of her life and her family expands and accelerates. And the cycle continues.

An alcoholic typically employs several defensive techniques that support and reinforce denial—that keep her from knowing the truth. First of all, she *rationalizes* her drinking, telling herself she doesn't drink so much more than others do, and that there are good reasons why she goes overboard on occasion. She also *blames* others for her excessive drinking, and for the abusive or neglectful things she does under the influence. The alcoholic often forgets the painful things that have happened to her and the destructive things she has done when she was drunk. She also makes *faulty comparisons* that help her to evade reality. As far as the alcoholic is concerned, a "drunk" is anyone who drinks more than she does.

It is very difficult for family members to believe that their alcoholic loved one is genuinely ignorant of the devastating impact of her drinking. Certainly some active alcoholics have greater self-awareness than others. However, many have extremely effective, *unconscious* denial mechanisms that massively distort physical and emotional reality. The chemicals that regularly saturate their central nervous systems only help these unconscious processes along.

The Spouse. Survival for the spouse in an alcoholic family depends on his ability to ensure his physical security and to suppress the intense emotional pain that threatens to overwhelm his self-worth and his hope for the future. In many instances, the spouse of an alcoholic adopts the same survival strategy employed by the alcoholic herself. That is, he alters his psychological and emotional reality. He may not drink to achieve this altered state, but rather use denial (and rationalization and blaming and forgetting) to reduce his disabling anxiety, preserve his self-esteem, and dampen his anger so that a violent confrontation with the alcoholic can be averted. Spouses of alcoholics who were forced to use denial to survive a dysfunctional family of origin are particularly prone to use this strategy when faced with the alcoholism of a marital partner.

A spouse in denial may be nearly as estranged from reality as the alcoholic. For one thing, he may believe that he can manage the alcoholic's drinking so that it will not pose a serious threat to the family. To this end, he will hide or destroy the drinker's supply of liquor, harass and punish her when she drinks, and avoid social occasions that present her with opportunities to drink. These efforts absorb great amounts of energy and time. They may effectively thwart the drinker on some occasions, but, unfortunately the will of a spouse is never enough to actually halt the progression of his partner's disease—unless he is able to move her into treatment (see chapter 5 and Appendix I).

Spouses also often believe that they can conceal their partner's compulsive drinking from children, relatives, friends, and employers. In their desperation to preserve the family's economic security, and the drinker's reputation, they lie to all these people about the reasons for the drinker's absences and her inability to function well in different situations. In some cases, the disease does advance extremely slowly and the drinker is able to do well at work and project an aura of normalcy that is convincing to outsiders. When most of the emotional fallout of this disease is contained within the family, friends and coworkers may be fooled. The family feels more financially and socially secure if it can pull this off, but a heavy toll is exacted for such mercies. The family that effectively hides its suffering has no hope of comfort, support, or assistance from outside. Family members remain completely alone with their fear, their anger, their hurt, and their shame. It is also true that the great majority of spouses who believe they are hiding compulsive drinking are fooling no one. No one confronts them with the truth because almost all their friends, relatives, and colleagues are just as embarrassed and confused about the disease of alcoholism as are the family members themselves.

Children frequently feign ignorance of the truth because they don't want to place further stress on their parents. But children do know, and they lose faith in parents who are unable to say what should be said, and do what must be done. Furthermore, like their parents, they ache for the comfort that is denied them when no one is permitted to speak the truth.

The Child

A LONG DARK NIGHT OF THE SOUL

The middle of the night—that's the worst time for me. I feel like I'm all alone in the world, everyone's left me, nobody cares. Some nights, I really start to panic. My heart starts to pound and the fear is really so strong that I think I'm going to lose it. I can't calm down until I call someone, make sure there's a friend, or a girl somewhere that cares whether I live or die.

Nights have been bad ever since I was a kid. I would wake up sometimes at 2 or 3 A.M. to the sound of my parents yelling at each other and threatening to split up. My father would be drunk and my mother would be hysterical, demanding to know where he'd been and who he'd been with. I'd lie there with a pillow over my head, trying to shut it all out, but worrying about what would happen if my Mom or Dad did actually leave.

I became this really insecure child. I hated to leave the house at all, and would even pretend I was sick so that I could stay home from school with my mother. A lot of kids take sick days to watch T.V. or read comic books, but I just wanted my mother to talk to me, to read to me, or sit and help me play with my toys. I drove her nuts following her around the house all the time. She hated it when I did that. She would get angry and tell me I had to learn to amuse myself, but I'd cry and say I couldn't. And I'd really pitch a fit if she tried to go out and leave me. Even at six or seven or eight, I can remember actually having temper tantrums when she wanted to meet her friends for lunch or golf. And it seemed to me like she was always going somewhere, that I could never get her to sit and be with me. Finally she started to drink, too, and it became totally impossible to reach her.

I know it seems like I'm okay now. I'm a writer, and I have to be alone. I actually manage to work alone all day and produce good stuff that sells. I have friends, and I date a fair amount, so everyone thinks I'm fairly normal, I guess. Except they must wonder about these weird phone calls they get in the middle of the night. But this fear—of being left—is always with me. It's always at the edge of things, waiting to get in if I turn off the typewriter and turn out the light. I never tell anyone this. I'm sure they don't want to hear it any more than my mother did. But I still feel like everybody's leaving me.

Keith—Age thirty-five

Familial alcoholism has been so well documented, and so vividly portrayed in the popular media in recent years, that almost everyone now knows that alcoholism is a family disease and that children are deeply and permanently affected by it. Just how deeply and how adversely they are affected depends on several factors that are discussed at length in this book. As a recovering parent, you must understand and remember that alcoholic drinking and destructive "wet" behaviors are not the gravest threat to the child in an addicted family. The principal problem for children of alcoholic and codependent parents is that *the family structure* so often breaks down in the face of chronic, heavy drinking.

A stable, hierarchical family structure frees children to be children. In the stable, well-organized family, parents lead and manage the family group. When an important problem is identified, they initiate and direct the process that will be followed in solving that problem. They are attuned and attentive to their children's needs for love, care, and emotional support. Parents in stable, well-functioning families are able to suspend their own emotional agendas when a child's need for emotional care and comfort is immediate and acute. In a "normal" family, parents create an atmosphere in which love and affection are easily expressed, but they do not expect to receive emotional or physical care from their children. They admire and encourage their children as unique, creative individuals and do not dispense rewards based on any child's capacity to bolster or compensate an ailing, struggling family. Most importantly, in an appropriately hierarchical family arrangement, parents protect their children from abuse and exploitation.

When parents remain in a parental role, even during periods of crisis and tumult in the family, children remain in an appropriately childish role. They follow, rather than lead, their parents. They do not regard themselves as the source of family crises and conflicts; therefore, they do not assume responsibility for the resolution of these problems. They direct their energy toward peers, play, and academic accomplishment.

Normal development in childhood depends, above all, on a child's ability and willingness to concentrate on "childish" things. Children *must* play, they *must* develop meaningful and mutually supportive peer relationships, and they *must* assimilate classroom lessons. This is how they acquire the knowledge and skills they need in order to work well, and love well, as adults. This is how they come to believe in themselves. This is how they acquire hope.

In alcoholic, codependent families, the normal, hierarchical division of labor and responsibility breaks down. Parents become preoccupied with alcohol and with self-preservation. They are unable to perceive and effectively cope with a pressing and threatening reality, and they cannot provide their children with adequate guidance, love, support, and protection. The promise of security, loyalty, and unconditional love, which is the mainstay of the relationship between parent and child, breaks down. When this happens, children cannot remain on a normal, or optimal, developmental path. Unsupported children in confusing and oppressive circumstances are forced into a defensive posture in which they, too, become obsessively concerned with self-protection. Many devote themselves to rescuing their parents and protecting their siblings. These unsupported children are often aggressively self-sufficient and may seem mature beyond their years. They are actually terrified of needing, or asking for, help, and they are vulnerable in many different ways. The following chapter explains exactly how a child's development is compromised when he must cope, all alone, with a parent's active alcoholism and the collapse of the family.

≡ 3 ≡

The Child in an
Alcoholic Family

The problems experienced by children who grow up in alcoholic families have been amply documented in the media in recent years. Although most people are happy enough to have the issue of familial alcoholism dragged out of the closet, many also feel saturated with information about this group. They feel that they now know more than they ever needed or wanted to know about alcoholism, "codependence," and children of alcoholics.

Although it seems that the story of the alcoholic family has been told and retold, hashed and rehashed, iterated, reiterated and rerun, most people are still lacking one crucial bit of information about children of alcoholics; they are all different.

When children from alcoholic families come together, they do find that they share certain feelings, certain problems, certain ways of perceiving the world, and certain ways of responding to relationships. They can easily identify with the experiences and reactions of the people they meet in support groups or therapy groups for children of alcoholics, or COA's, because they have had similar experiences and they have, on occasion, felt similar things. But most adult children of alcoholics who spend an extended period of time in such groups come to see that their own feelings and their own lives are in many ways unique. They find that they are more or less depressed than their cohorts; that they are better adjusted at work, or that they struggle more in romantic relationships; that they face their problems with a greater sense of hope, or with a deeper feeling of despair.

Children of alcoholics differ from one another because alcoholic families differ from one another. Some children in alcoholic families grow up with many siblings; others grow up alone. Some children are very young when a parent develops alcoholism, while some are nearly grown when this occurs. Some children live in families in which one parent remains sober and supportive, whereas others grow up with two alcoholic parents. Some children are able to escape to the home of a kindly relative. Others join Alateen. Some families pursue an organized program of recovery, whereas some families fall apart completely.

Alcoholism has been called "the great masquerader" because individual drinkers react differently to alcohol's toxic properties and develop different symptoms. Families react differently to the problem of parental alcoholism, and children are affected as much and perhaps more by the nature of the family's reaction than they are affected by the drinking itself. The most critical question for children in alcoholic families is whether they will be supported, guided, and loved while the family is in crisis. Where the center holds, and at least one parent continues to serve as the child's compassionate guide, interpreting the family's difficult experience, and struggling to manage it, the outlook is bright. As the last section of this chapter makes clear, some children actually gain strength and confidence as they deal with the problem of a parent's alcoholism.

The first part of this chapter, however, details some of the adverse outcomes experienced by some children in alcoholic families. Children with alcoholic and codependent parents frequently have problems with

- *The formation of self-identity*
- *The development of self-esteem*

They may also experience difficulties with

- *Emotional awareness and self-expression*
- *Physical health*
- *Intellectual development*
- *Academic performance*

The next few sections describe the kinds of problems that may arise in each of these areas. But, once again, there is no "COA syndrome"—no single effect that each child in an alcoholic home is bound to experience. The problems described in the following sections occur with some frequency in children of alcoholic and codependent parents, but some children experience just a few of these effects whereas others experience a great many. Some children are hurt very badly and display marked dysfunction, whereas others feel only mild and transient distress. Indeed, some children in alcoholic homes develop at a normal pace, and even show some gains as a result of negotiating unusual challenges at home.

Children are at greatest risk when a parent's alcoholism is chronic and untreated, and when there is no adult at home, or nearby, to protect them, or to help them understand why they and their family are suffering so.

Effects on Self-Identity

Chapter 2 described alcoholism as an illness that has some hereditary base, but that is also influenced by psychological and environmental factors. In some way, all of life is like this. We are born with, and develop according to, some internal plan. However, this plan includes many contingencies. It may expand or contract, and its objectives and emphases may shift, in response to cues and conditions in the environment.

A child is born, we believe, with certain biological givens: a particular temperamental disposition; a set of native endowments and limitations that influence intellectual and physical performance; and a constitution that tends to be either robust or relatively delicate. There is disagreement as to just when children first begin to experience a feeling of selfhood, and about how much of the self, or personality, is determined by heredity rather than environment. Most authorities would agree that, although there may be an inherited "core" self, a child's personality is malleable and much of it is formed in response to people and conditions in the family.

How Parental Character and Behavior
Influence Personality Development

Children's personalities are powerfully influenced by the personalities and behavior of their parents. Children actually incorporate broad portions of parental character. We hear a great deal about the "inner child," who dwells at the center of each adult. Well, every child carries within himself the image and voice of an "internal parent." This parent speaks to the child about the nature of the world he must face, and guides him as he acts, and judges his acts in this world. It takes a great deal of time and experience for children to objectively evaluate and reject irrational beliefs that their parents hold and to repudiate destructive acts they commit. Therefore, dysfunctional patterns of coping and reacting are incorporated along with adaptive, constructive practices.

Consider first a positive example of the way in which children internalize parental character. Imagine a child who is naturally timid and cautious, but who is raised by an adventurous, supremely self-confident, and emotionally supportive parent. This parent is able to accept the fact that her child's temperament is different from her own; therefore she is able to be compassionate about her youngster's fears. At the same time, she uses her own spirit of adventure to reassure and guide the child through scary situations. She doesn't demean her child when he is frightened at the playground. Instead, she says something like, "That is a big slide. I'll bet it looks pretty scary from the top. When you're ready to try it though, I'll be waiting at the bottom to catch you." On other occasions the parent demonstrates, through her own eager pursuit of adventure, that novelty and challenge can be met with excitement as well as with apprehension.

Years of experience and interaction with this kind of parent will cause her boldness, as well as her patience and sensitivity, to become embedded in her child's personality. Eventually, these characteristics will become a fundamental element of the child's own *self*-image, and will exist side by side with his inborn reticence.

As the child grows up, he will be able to activate his good "internal parent" whenever he starts to become anxious. If he finds himself in a tight spot, our reluctant adventurer will tell himself the things his parent used to tell him when he was hesitant and afraid: "This is hard. I *am* scared. But soon, I'll be ready." He will replay, in his mind, the challenges he dared and mastered with his parent's support. Heartened by images of his parent's courage, and faith in him, and fortified by his recollection of past victories, the child will advance to meet the current test, despite the fear he feels.

The internal image of an accepting, unanxious, and supportive parent is absolutely essential if a child is to approach the world with a feeling of trust and optimism. Once again, this image, which is initially a memory of a parent-child interaction, is reinforced over time and repeated experience with the parent. Eventually, it becomes a fundamental and powerful element of the child's own self, and self-image. This is one important way in which children come to see themselves as capable and admirable human beings.

Alcoholic and alcohol-preoccupied parents often project a very different image to their children. When they are too terrified to face the fact of a destructive addiction, they tend to retreat from reality and may withdraw, emotionally from their children. If they regard the world as indifferent and even hostile to their problems, they are likely to insist that the family exist in a fearful, isolated, and secretive relation to the larger community. Their shame and their need to deny the existence of the disease that torments them can lead them to blame others, including their children, for the breakdown of the family.

Young children are in no position to reject such harmful attitudes and behaviors. They have little basis for comparison, and they are programmed at birth for survival, which means they more or less automatically follow the lead of adults with whom they live. Therefore, a child in an alcoholic family is likely to assimilate into his own self-image a fearful, shamed, and retreating parent who feels critical and suspicious of others, including him. Unless his native temperament pulls him powerfully in another direction, he, too, will become fearful, defensive, and harshly critical of himself. If children repeatedly observe parents physically hurting one another, they will also incorporate images of abusiveness and violence into their own personalities, and may begin to behave aggressively toward others. If they have been the target of physical abuse at home, they will grow to believe that they deserve to be treated cruelly by others.

Rewards, Punishments, and Sheer Necessity Also Influence Personality

Parents also influence the final form of a child's personality by rewarding, ignoring, or punishing certain behaviors and attitudes the child naturally displays. Unfortunately some parents, when they are in extreme emotional pain, expect to be bolstered and sustained by their children. They are attentive and loving when their children behave in a nurturing way, or when they do things that provide their parents with an ego boost, but they are disengaged, and even hostile, when the children pursue their own interests.

WHOSE LIFE IS IT, ANYWAY?

One father, who used alcohol to assuage the feelings of deprivation and shame he felt about a childhood spent in poverty and powerlessness, was determined to raise a child who would become an influential and wealthy doctor. His eldest son had an affinity, perhaps a genius, for music, but was punished and ridiculed for his efforts to fulfill this talent.

Daniel became devoted to fulfilling his father's dreams. He pushed himself to complete a degree in chemistry despite his modest skills in science and math, and allowed his music to become a halfhearted avocation. This young man was even accepted to medical school, but the pain engendered by repeated acts of self-denial led him to develop a severe dependency on cocaine and alcohol. He left medical school, completed a rehabilitation program, and then entered psychotherapy, where he began the difficult work of distinguishing his own interests and needs from those of his father.

Sometimes sheer necessity dictates the focus of a child's behavior, and the ultimate form of his character. Parents become so ill that they almost fully abandon their roles as caretakers and guides for their children. Youngsters who identify strongly with depressed or delinquent "runaway" elements in their parents' personalities withdraw emotionally or rebel and fight when this happens. Others attempt to fill the breach.

The "parentified" child will struggle to perform the functions that parents have relinquished. He will cook the meals, clean the house, comfort and discipline his siblings, and try as hard as he can to bring a sense of normalcy and stability to family life. As he does so, he is likely to neglect personal interest and native talents. He may even begin to shun peer relationships, to neglect academic responsibilities, and to defer vocational ambitions. Natural curiosity and playfulness inevitably decline as such a child focuses narrowly on the grueling task of shepherding the family through one more day of struggle and apprehension. Such heroic effort calls on, and further develops, useful qualities such as perseverance, determination, and self-reliance. These particular characteristics are quite prominent in many children of alcoholic and codependent parents.

The role of family hero, or rescuer, however, tends to be incompatible with other traits that are important for a happy adjustment. For example, children of alcoholics who take on a great many parenting functions may have a hard time identifying, or even feeling, their longing for love and emotional support. These needs have been disappointed so often that, for the sake of psychological survival, they have been blocked from awareness. Many children of alcoholics also have a difficult time trusting or becoming emotionally intimate with others. Once again, they have learned that to rely on others is to risk crushing disappointment.

THE MOVING TARGET

I worked so hard to keep my mother going. I worked all the time as a child. And I still work all the time. Ten-hour days, twelve-hour days, fourteen-hour days. I just keep moving, you know. What did the White Rabbit say? "No time to say hello—goodbye!"

If you wanted to get to know me, wanted to know anything significant about me or my past, you'd have to clear a few hurdles first. You'd have to be perfectly understanding, perfectly sympathetic, perfectly accepting and perfectly tolerant. Well, you can see what I'm doing, of course. No one ever gives all the right answers, so no one is ever admitted to the inner circle. I never have to say the magic words. "My mother is a drunk and a dope fiend. She lives in a shack, and I secretly believe I'm a derelict just like she is."

Would my friends respect me if they knew those things? Would any man want to come near me? I'll probably never know. I'll just go on hiding and feeling like the fake I am. Actually I won't really feel that. I'll just keep working.

Jillian—Age thirty-eight

Effects on Self-Esteem

Children from alcoholic families often have great difficulty thinking well of themselves. Some are exceedingly successful at school and work, but because they are perfectionists, they feel like failures when they are unable to win *every* competition and "ace" *every* test. Others feel so completely incompetent and worthless that they barely try when any sort of challenge presents itself.

There are three major threats to a child's self-esteem in an alcoholic family. First, many alcoholic and codependent parents have terribly low self-esteem. When this is the case, children assimilate into their personalities the image of an anxious, self-critical, self-disappointed parent. This powerfully affects a youngster's self-perception, as noted previously.

Second, parents who are struggling with alcoholism in themselves or in a partner are under constant, heavy emotional pressure. Many grow to feel incompetent and ashamed about their inability to beat this complicated and destructive disease. As time goes on, their feelings of frustration and shame escalate to such a degree that it becomes too painful for them to continue to look inside themselves for the answers to their problems. They begin, not deliberately, but unconsciously, to relieve the internal pressure they feel by viewing others as the source of their continuing difficulty. Thus, a mother who feels worthless and contemptible for her inability to stop drinking tells her son, "You're lazy and useless. Why don't you get out of the house and try to do something to help this family?"

Or, a father who believes he is weak and stupid because he is unable to solve the riddle of his wife's alcoholism, questions his daughter, who is an honor-roll student, "How could you possibly get a B in Chemistry? Don't you have the brains to figure out the tough courses? Or are you only able to get the easy stuff like English and French?"

Once again, it takes time, experience, and exposure to other adults, before children develop a great deal of insight into their parents' problems. Most children see themselves pretty much as their parents see them, and even though they may amend this view as they grow older, a parent's perspective always influences a child's basic feeling about himself. If a parent's attitude toward a child is fundamentally negative, the child will have to fight to develop and preserve a feeling of basic worth.

THE NOWHERE MAN

Alan was a gifted young man who was unable to use his considerable talents, because his personal aspirations conflicted with his strong desire to comfort and sustain his alcoholic mother.

Alan felt great pressure from his mother to be "a good boy," and a success at nearly everything he tried. His extraordinary intellectual gifts made school a natural arena for the achievement of academic honors and prizes that he hoped would cheer and bolster his mother, who often seemed depressed and angry.

Even when he moved to the top of class, however, and became president of the student council, Alan sensed that his mother was never really satisfied. Her faint praise and eager anticipation of his next, even grander accomplishment, left Alan feeling chronically anxious, and dissatisfied with himself.

And there was another, somewhat paradoxical, dimension to this mother's expectations of her son. While Alan was supposed to be a paragon of achievement and virtue at school, he was often scapegoated at home. His mother often bullied and ridiculed him when they were alone, and she was harshly critical of his interest in various humanistic and spiritual movements. She warned him that she would feel disgraced if he chose to become an artist, or a minister, and failed to advance the family's prominent name in the world of business.

Alan graduated from a liberal arts program at a top university (again, with honors), and when he did, he moved to another coast to start a life of his own. He found it impossible to begin something that truly was his own however. When he took a low-paying job as a social worker in a poor section of town, he was tormented by the sound of his mother's voice in his head, telling him that he was a failure and a shame to his family. When he tried to complete an application for business school, however, he heard another voice, from deep inside himself, begging him not to "sell out" and give up on the commitment he truly felt to serve humankind.

Alan became hamstrung by the battle raging inside. Unable to enroll in a business program, and too guilty and fearful to make a commitment to study for the clergy, he took a humdrum job in government. He struggled against the urge to spend most days in bed, and, when he was able to make it to work, he spent more guilty hours doodling on a legal pad, and scribbling, "You are a disgrace."

The third threat to self-esteem in an alcoholic family has ironically, to do with a child's natural egocentrism. Because they are cognitively immature, and lack experience with the world, younger children see themselves as the center and source of all things. For a time, they believe they are all-powerful. Thus, children in alcoholic families blame themselves for their parents' pain. They assume they have done something to hurt their mother and father, and condemn themselves for their failure to heal their parents and restore the family. If parents, in their anguish and need, frequently turn to their children for support, this unfortunate view of the world is reinforced and tends to persist even as the children mature in other ways. Many children from alcoholic families grow up to achieve enormous worldly success, but find it impossible to feel pride in their accomplishments. They feel guilty and deficient because their parents still drink.

Effects on Emotional Development

A child who has been repeatedly disappointed and hurt by a parent has to find a way to manage his painful memories of that parent, and his intense feelings about her as well. If the child has access to another adult who can reassure and support him, who will protect him from emotional and physical violence, and who can help him to understand his struggle with the parent who is ill, there is a good chance that he will manage his pain. He will eventually grasp the idea that his parent is ill. He will see that this affects her capacity to love and care for him, and he will accept that her destructive acts are neither his fault nor his responsibility. At the same time, the child will use the relationship with his positive adult to build up an image of himself as strong, capable, and worthy of love and care. In the long run, this child may be more grounded, more resilient, and more mature than his age-mates who were not challenged by a difficult home situation.

In many instances, however, children of alcoholics have no positive adult to shield them from abuse or to help them master powerful, painful feelings about their parents. Without an adult guide, a child in an alcoholic family can not truly "manage" his situation so that his development will continue in a normal, healthy manner. Still, the child must find some way to survive his problematic family. He must devise some strategy that will enable him to hold himself and his family together, to contain and minimize damage to his self-esteem, and to develop whatever skills and abilities he can to make his way in the larger world outside the family.

In the last chapter we discussed how active alcoholics and actively codependent spouses of alcoholics "survive" in a chaotic situation by denying important aspects of physical and emotional reality. Once again, the denial of reality by alcoholics and their partners is not a simple matter of lying or distorting the truth. Rather, it involves an actual and profound loss of self-awareness that serves to reduce psychic pain.

Children in alcoholic families, as they develop their own survival strategy, observe the ways in which their parents cope with pain. Furthermore, as they are children, they have a built-in and easily accessed capacity for fantasy and illusion. And so, the great majority of unsupported children in alcoholic families handle pain exactly as their parents do: They distort or obliterate vast portions of their personal reality.

Denial and Repression in Childhood

A child under severe, chronic stress, who has no adult guide, finds that it is his memory, his anger, and his longing for love and care that bring him the most grief. His memories are unbearable because they contain images of the suffering that he and his beloved parents have experienced. All of the arguments, the emotional and physical violence, and the broken promises are recorded and held in memory. When there is no grown-up to help a child make sense of these images, or to show him how he can overcome the experiences they represent, accurate memory becomes an intolerable burden.

The child finds his anger intolerable because it feels intense, and savage, and he fears that, if he expresses it, it will trigger more chaotic behavior in those he loves, destroying them and him as well.

The child's yearning for love, and for emotional warmth and support, is unbearable to him simply because it is so often frustrated. In some dysfunctional homes expressions of need are even criticized or punished by parents.

The unsupported child in an alcoholic home buries images of painful encounters with his parents. He manages to "forget" his feelings of hurt, vulnerability, and longing. He must do this in order to avoid being overwhelmed by pain. When you ask him, he says that things at home are "fine." He says that *he* is "fine". For the most part, he believes this—just as his mother, who hides a bottle of gin in her briefcase, another in her desk drawer, and still another in the trunk of her car, believes that she is fine.

These children often appear fine to the uninformed outsider. They usually seem okay to their families, as well. This is because so many of them develop an attitude of toughness, confidence, and self-sufficiency that effectively conceals the underlying condition of hurt and frustrated need. Even when a child is so troubled by his home situation, and so identified with an alcoholic parent's impulsive behavior that he acts up in school and gets into trouble with authorities, he is liable to appear mean and angry, not hurt.

A child with a more introverted disposition who is in pain, but cannot express it, may withdraw into schoolwork or fantasy play in order to distract himself from feelings of hurt and loneliness. Even though he is quiet and uncommunicative, however, his cooperative and submissive behavior toward adults may convince them that he, too, is "fine" and content in his solitary state.

The Impact of Denial and Repression

The first casualty of a deliberate campaign to "forget" bad experiences and painful feelings is the child's energy reserve. The child who swallows his need, represses and denies his longing, forgets traumatic events, and distorts his awareness of, and reactions to, a deteriorating family situation never really succeeds in eradicating his internal pain. He only moves it about in his mind, trying to find a niche where it can be confined and controlled indefinitely. His intense and ongoing effort to keep his inner truth at bay depletes him emotionally. This leads inevitably to some kind of emotional, social, or behavioral trouble.

Loss of Depth and Meaning in Relationships. In many cases, the child's ability to function socially with his peers is badly compromised. Even when the unsupported child is able to find the time, energy, and motivation to acquire friends, he is likely to feel unfulfilled in their company. If he is unable to be honest with himself, he won't be able to form a candid, open relationship with a friend, and he will find himself frustrated at the lack of depth in his relationships. Moreover, his friendships may intensify, rather than relieve, his feeling of internal pressure. Some children regard peer relationships as another arena in which they must be careful not to feel or say too much. If they are receiving little, or no, emotional support at home, they tend to believe that it is normal to be left alone with pain and self-doubt. They do not expect friends to listen or to comfort them, and they may even believe that their friends would criticize or abandon them if they asked for their help. Even in the course of a long afternoon with a best buddy, the unsupported child is careful to keep his own counsel. Of course, this only deepens his feeling of emotional alienation and exhaustion.

MARIE

Marie's father was physically and verbally abusive to his wife and children when he drank. He occasionally brawled with neighbors as well, and everyone in the family felt humiliated by his behavior. No one felt able to openly express their shame, however, and no one spoke of feeling angry, or hurt, either.

Marie's mother was chronically depressed, probably as a result of her husband's chronic drinking. She never acknowledged his alcoholism, and never objected to his brutality toward her or their children. She would only shrug and say, "That's just the way he is." She became angry and critical when the children dared to complain about the quality of family life, deriding them for their "whining," or their "babyish tantrums." She prided herself on her emotional reserve and dignity. She expected her children to bear up in similar fashion.

Marie was the oldest child, and possessed of a very tender heart. She felt her mother's unexpressed shame and sadness very deeply. She never complained, as she could see how this upset her mother, and she tried hard to reduce the pressure her mother felt. She eagerly pitched in with family chores and tended lovingly to her younger brothers and sisters. Unfortunately, her mother was so depressed and emotionally withdrawn that she was never able to thank Marie for her efforts. In fact, she would often shame Marie by expressing disappointment and redoing any task that seemed to have been completed imperfectly. Marie would swallow her hurt when this happened, and offer to try again.

Marie escaped to a loveless marriage at age eighteen, but she never spoke to family or friends of the pain this relationship brought her. Even her best friend believed that the childhood sweethearts had formed an idyllic union. In reality, Marie's husband was a demanding perfectionist who never felt gratified by her efforts to please. He was also unfaithful to her, and an irresponsible parent to their two young children. Marie tried to emulate her mother's response to abuse and neglect in a marital relationship. She repressed her longing for love and concealed her anger and disappointment. She presented a convincing, but totally false, face of calm and unconcern to the world for nearly ten years. Then, when her husband left her for another woman, and she had no means, and no one to whom to express her despair, she tried to kill herself with an overdose of sleeping pills and alcohol.

Emotional Instability and the Development of Compulsive Behaviors. Chronic repression and denial of emotion exhaust a child and deplete his relationships. They also unbalance him. This is because human beings are social animals. Their feelings naturally and endlessly seek release, as well as the acknowldgement of a compassionate listener. Many unsupported children labor to contain their distress and their profound need, with compulsive exercise, compulsive work, or compulsive eating. Still, their emotions press upward and outward. Sometimes a stressful event or interaction triggers a sudden release of pent-up feeling. There is an unexpected and startling outburst of anger or delinquency, or a precipitous plunge into depression. The hidden pain is exposed, however briefly. Most of the time, however, when an unsupported child senses a rush of conscious pain, he quickly escalates his involvement with activities that serve as an effective hedge against his pain. He begins to "binge" on food, fantasy, computer games, or exercise when stress builds up and he feels at risk for an emotional outburst. Some children employ this strategy throughout childhood, and continue to rely on it as adults. If they are compulsive about socially sanctioned activities, such as schoolwork or sports, other people may never detect the delicate and difficult "balancing act" that is going on internally. Parents, friends, and teachers will assume that everything is fine, and praise the achievements that flow from such concentrated effort.

A DOUBLE LIFE

Children will try to repress and deny their longing for care when a parent cannot provide it. But this effort destabilizes the personality, impairs emotional functioning, and disorders personal relationships.

Diana's father died, after a prolonged illness, when she was eight years old. Her parents never discussed the nature of this illness with Diana, and little was said about his death after it occurred. There was no opportunity for her to grieve, openly, with her mother, and thus, no chance that she could be comforted about the loss of her father. Mother's alcoholism accelerated rapidly after Diana's father's death, and Diana was often left in the care of her paternal grandmother. Diana raged at her grandmother about this further abandonment, and demanded to see her mother. On occasion, she cried hysterically for her mother's care. But her mother could not respond. Too often, she could not even hear Diana's cries. She had already passed out in her bedroom from an afternoon of drinking.

Diana often feigned illness so that she might remain home from school, and share her mother's company during the day. When the two were together, however, it was still impossible for Diana to get the love and comfort she craved. Her mother would drink, and she would reproach Diana harshly if she complained about this, or if she asked for help or care the mother felt unable to give. One afternoon, Diana's mother found Diana emptying liquor bottles into the kitchen sink. She shrieked at the child, "I'm not hurting *you*, Diana!"

But, of course, Diana *was* hurt. She was particularly harmed by the failure to grieve for her father, and by her mother's inability to acknowledge her legitimate needs for love and support. She began to feel guilty and ashamed of needing her mother, and did everything she could to become the self-contained, self-sufficient child her mother seemed to want her to be. She stopped complaining, and pretended to be happy. She did not speak to the family, or to close friends about her mother's drinking, and she began to reproach herself when feelings of sadness, grief, or anger would break through. She told herself the things her mother told her, and thought herself spoiled, selfish, and infantile for wanting more comfort and support.

Self-criticism diverted Diana from her grief and helped her to continue in the role of dutiful and self-sufficient daughter. As an adolescent, Diana discovered that cigarettes and alcohol were also an effective means of boosting her mood, and she used these freely. She thought of the girl who smoked and drank as "bad Diana," and had a hard time understanding the connection between this part of herself, and the good girl who did so well in school, and was, at most other times, conventional, well-adjusted, and reasonably carefree.

After college, Diana married a successful businessman and had two children. She eventually earned a graduate degree and went on to build a successful business of her own. Her colleagues and clients found her extraordinarily likeable and competent. However, she continued to experience the pressure of her unacknowledged pain about the past. There were periodic bouts of depression and intense anxiety. Diana tried to manage these episodes as she always had—by denying the pain, working harder, and trying to shame herself into a more becoming attitude and posture. Since she had married a man who was as hostile to her longing for emotional support and comfort as her mother had been, her despair was more intense than ever, and more irresistible, and she began to use cocaine, in addition to nicotine and alcohol, in an effort to escape her most negative feelings. Ultimately, she came to depend on the regular intake of drugs and alcohol for her "show" of congeniality and optimism to go on. And, in time, she was every bit as addicted as her mother had been.

Unlike her mother, Diana was able to acknowledge how hurtful her compulsive behavior was, both to herself and her children. She entered treatment, and joined Alcoholics Anonymous, where she became sober and began to face, and grieve, the tragedies of her childhood.

The "Imposter Syndrome". The praise that the "compulsive overachiever" receives is often a valuable boon to his self-esteem, but, once again, the child pays a price for his successful deception. At some level, he knows that he is not entirely what he appears to be. He knows that there are things beneath the surface that no one else ever sees—feelings and memories that he regards as dangerous, shameful, and even monstrous. He concludes that he does not quite deserve the praise he is receiving, and so, he discounts it and fails to receive its full benefit. He develops a new fear that one day he will be publicly exposed as an imposter. He redoubles his efforts to hide and "forget" that which lurks beneath the surface. This causes the distressing images and tormenting feelings to press ever harder for relief and resolution. This, in turn, fuels further compulsive behavior. Like his parents, the unsupported child becomes trapped in a self-destructive cycle of escalating pain, declining self-worth, increasing denial, and accelerating compulsivity.

Alienation and Self-Hatred. In the end, the unsupported ch
to afford accurate memory or authentic feeling, becomes estr
alienated from himself. He is not quite sure who he is, or wha
since he so often dissembles. He is sure, however, that he do
himself very much. He particularly dislikes and fears the part o. ..mself
that craves love and care from others. This is the part that has led him,
time and again, to ask for support and affection. And time and again he
has been turned away by parents who are too hurt themselves to
respond. The unsupported, chronically stressed child from an alcoholic
family tries not to feel bad and not to need any help, so that he can
avoid this crushing disappointment. When he finds that he can't stop
the flow of longing, he becomes deeply angry with himself. He may feel
so desperate to stop wanting, and needing others, that he begins to punish himself whenever he becomes aware of, or impulsively expresses, his
need. Some children punish themselves with harsh and unrelenting self-
criticism. Some start to hit or cut themselves, or become involved with
"friends" who are cruel to them. Their self-esteem continues to plunge.
Depression and anxiety mount.

Effects on Health

When adults who grew up in alcoholic families look back on their
childhood experiences, they often say that they always felt frightened
when they were young. They say that it was impossible to relax, and enjoy
peaceful, happy moments in their families, because they knew that these
periods of calm were only temporary conditions. At any minute, the alcoholic parent might take a drink, and all hell would break loose. Many
children from alcoholic families remember remaining perpetually
braced for such an eventuality.

The effort to remain constantly vigilant and emotionally prepared for
calamity places an enormous strain on a child. The pressure is, of course,
much greater if he knows that he will be alone when disaster finally does
strike. A portion of the pressure a child feels in this kind of situation is
physical. The body undergoes actual biochemical changes when the brain
senses an imminent threat, and many children in alcoholic homes feel
threatened all the time. The physical strain of life in an alcoholic home
places children at risk for physical illness. Some children are especially
vulnerable to a physical breakdown: Children who are physically endangered in their homes, those who are constitutionally less hearty, and those
who receive inadequate nourishment or medical care because of their
parents' illness are particularly likely to develop stress-related illnesses.

Effects on Intellectual and Academic Development and Performance

Academic tasks are often neglected when children become preoccupied with serious family problems. Children in alcoholic families may also be affected by other conditions that decrease intellectual potential and hinder school performance.

Insufficient Stimulation

Normal intellectual development depends, to some degree, on the quality and amount of cognitive and physical stimulation that a child receives in early life. Exposure to literature and music is probably the first thing we think of when we imagine a "stimulating" home. As valuable as such exposure is, however, it is only one aspect of an interesting and challenging family environment. During infancy and toddlerhood, it is also important that a child be stimulated by a variety of interesting sights and sounds, and by his parents' touch as well. Some parents feel too overwhelmed or too depressed to hold and play with their young children. They don't make it a point to carry their baby about so that the baby can be excited about the shapes and lights and sounds of the world inside and outside his home. Therefore, the baby never has to make the effort to organize and analyze novel sensory situations. This may delay the baby's development of certain cognitive functions and reduce his intellectual performance and potential.

Overstimulation

On the other hand, some children are easily overstimulated, and some homes are too loud and too disorganized so that a child cannot make sense of his environment. This can also create problems, since a child may have to withdraw in order to protect himself from being bombarded with stimuli he is too young to organize and manage. A child who withdraws into the world of fantasy and self-preoccupation too easily, and too often, will also miss important opportunities to learn and develop.

Parents who have the energy to tune in to their children will more easily assess their child's reaction to the situation the child is in. The parents will know his temperament and notice if he becomes withdrawn or agitated, because he's feeling too little or too much. The parents will know that their infant is engaged and appropriately excited by his surroundings because he appears absorbed and curious as he intently observes the action around him. They will be satisfied that their older child is feeling comfortable with his situation when he watches for a while, and then tries to "do something" with his environment, interacting in some way with the people nearby or touching and attempting to use the materials at hand.

If parents are having a great deal of difficulty managing their own feelings and reactions, however, they may not be able to help when their children are feeling uncomfortable with the outer environment. The youngsters will have to defend themselves as best they can. And when they are defending, they're not learning.

Fetal Alcohol Syndrome and Fetal Alcohol Effects

Some children of alcoholic mothers are born with fetal alcohol syndrome (FAS) because their mothers continued to drink during pregnancy. Fetal alcohol syndrome is described more fully in chapter 9. It is marked by certain physical characteristics and intellectual deficits that are caused by alcohol crossing the placental barrier and entering the bloodstream and central nervous system of the developing fetus. Children with fetal alcohol syndrome show certain physical anomalies, and they have difficulty learning from experience. They experience serious problems in adjusting to school and family life. Some children do not develop fullblown FAS, but show instead fetal alcohol effects (FEA). (See chapter 9.)

Conclusion

Alcoholism is a potent and destructive family disease. When a parent is actively alcoholic, and the family disavows and conceals this fact, all phases of the child's development may be affected. The risk of severe psychological injury is greatest in those families in which the drinking is chronic and severe and overall family structure begins to collapse. In many cases, the family becomes so ill that there is no organized, sustained effort to resolve, or even address, the alcoholism. Parents begin to abuse or neglect their children; no one tries to help youngsters comprehend their parents' behavior; and the feeling of stress and impending calamity is nearly unrelieved from day to day. The prognosis for a child in this sort of environment is grim indeed.

Invulnerable Children?

However, many children of alcoholic parents do grow up to be healthy, well-adjusted adults. They not only survive the difficult circumstances of their childhoods, but seem to flourish in response to the very struggles that defeat and destroy other children. These adult "survivors" acknowledge the traumas of early life and have a good deal of insight into the various strategies and techniques they employed to master these problems. Since their view of the past is relatively undistorted, they are able to learn from it. They feel enlightened, rather than encumbered by their childhood experiences. Most important, they are not addicted to alcohol or other mood-altering substances and activities.

Social scientists and mental health professionals are greatly interested in the resilient veterans of alcoholic families. They hope someday to identify the factors that enable some children to prosper in oppressive circumstances. Some of these theorists speculate that children with a strong constitution and a broad capacity for faith and hope are virtually immune to the destructive effects of parental alcoholism.

A child's ability to sustain feelings of hope and confidence about the future is a powerful determinant of his ability to survive and grow in an alcoholic family. Some children do seem to be endowed with a natural optimism, as well as the will to persevere in the face of extraordinary challenge. *However, no child is immune to the pain of losing a parent, or to the pain of being abused or neglected by a parent.* Every child who must cope with chronic, debilitating illness in a parent is stressed and hurt to some degree. The stress is heightened if the illness causes frightening changes in mood and behavior, as alcoholism does.

The Importance of Hope

Whereas hope and a solid sense of self-worth cannot prevent a child in an alcoholic home from being hurt, these attributes do help children avoid serious emotional illness, even in the face of protracted, intense stress at home.

The optimistic, self-confident child does not feel responsible for Mom or Dad's alcoholism, and he does not believe that he or his family can be destroyed by it. He does view the drinking as a serious problem, but he understands that it is one his parents must solve. He knows that he must develop strategies to cope with the erratic, sometimes abusive behavior of his drinking parent, but he believes he will be guided and supported by his sober parent as he faces this problem. The hopeful child who is convinced of his own value is less preoccupied with his parent's drinking, so he is able to do the things that children in "normal" families do—play with friends and learn from schoolwork. Therefore, he is much more likely to develop "normally" and become a resourceful and self-confident adult.

Inspiration Begins at Home

Few children are born with this kind of boundless optimism and unconquerable self-esteem. Children derive feelings of trust, hope, and self-assurance from their day-to-day dealings with fundamentally healthy parents: parents who face conflict honestly and directly, who strive to uphold and transmit a set of humane values, who experience and express a full range of human feeling, and who protect their children.

Just as children naturally reach out for love, affirmation, and care from their parents, parents long to provide the security and emotional nourishment their children need. But it is hard enough for a parent to remain honest, stable, and emotionally responsive in the face of the common, ordinary calamities human beings face every day. Parents in alcoholic families are challenged to do this and more. During the tumultuous, painful period of personal recovery from alcoholism and codependence, they must confront their children's pain directly and honestly. They must provide their children with the information, guidance, and support youngsters need in order to understand and cope with alcoholism as a disease. At a time when they feel they have very little to give, recovering parents must find a way to give more time, more tolerance, more understanding, and more love than ever before. The aim of this book is to make this mission possible; to explain how recovering parents can become "therapeutic" parents and create an emotionally honest, emotionally stable, and emotionally responsive home environment in which children can heal and in which they can learn to master the challenge of parental alcoholism.

= 4 =

The Therapeutic Parent

Ahealthy parent is a beacon for a child and a safe harbor in times of crisis for the family or the community. She is also a protective shield, a barrier to absorb and reduce intense and potentially traumatic pain that arises as a result of physical injury or as a consequence of an illness that strikes the body or the spirit. She is a stronghold of love and support within which a child may explore and test himself, and the sturdy base upon which he may ultimately found his own character.

Parents in an actively alcoholic or recovering family must provide yet another dimension of support for their children, since in most cases, these youngsters have sustained significant damage to the structure of the self and to their self-esteem. Parents who raise healthy children in an alcoholic home are "therapeutic" parents. They are able to marshal and apply a variety of resources inside and outside the family in such a way as to restore their children to a state of overall health and prevent additional damage. In a sense, they are able to construct an emotional safety net for their children, who may have fallen badly out of phase with standard timetables for development and adjustment.

The Safety Net

A SONG FOR GARY

I know now what I didn't know then. My mother was mixing pills and booze and that's why she never changed her clothes, why she never even got out of bed some days, why she died. I think I was just in second grade when she really fell apart. I was scared to death about what could be wrong with her, and probably pretty angry at my father because he didn't seem to be helping her. I sort of went on strike at that point. I wouldn't eat much, and a lot of days, I wouldn't get out of bed either. I just refused to go to school. My father took over though. He would sit there on the bed awhile and read to me until I was ready to get dressed. Then he'd make breakfast, and then—he'd get his guitar! He was a musician, and he'd play every song I could think to ask for, or that he knew I really liked until I had eaten a little bit. Then he'd drive me to school. And he was always there at three o'clock to pick me up. I look back now, and of course, I wish he'd figured out some way to save her. But then I think, "Well, Gary, at least he saved you."

Gary—Age twenty-three

Many children from alcoholic homes are immersed in a struggle to survive, and so they withdraw from activities and relationships outside the family. Therefore, they never develop the emotional and psychological skills they need to prosper in the "normal" world. Although different children, from different alcoholic families, experience and express their pain in different ways, they all suffer enormous anxiety, confusion, and frustration when they sense that they have lost, or are losing, their foothold in the so-called "normal" world. They all long to find a tender and forgiving point of contact with an existence that seems to be slipping irrevocably away. However, most deeply fear that there can be no soft landing, that there is nothing below them as they fall but more thin air.

Unfortunately, in many alcoholic homes, parents never turn to face their problems, and children do fall completely away from the world of healthy relationships and creative self-expression. As a recovering parent, you have decided to heal yourself and you will want to help your child resolve the pain that he is experiencing on account of the "family" disease. You want to understand his struggle and formulate an effective plan for repairing the damage that has been done. The task seems complex and intimidating. How can you fashion and cast a net to break a child's fall from hope and hold him in a position of emotional security where he can begin to rebuild his sense of self-identity and self-worth?

The safety net that you hold for your child will inevitably have flaws in its fabric. It will not prevent every bruise to the spirit, nor will it heal every fracture of the psyche. Gary's father didn't understand his wife's illness and left her to the care of her physician, who treated her "depression" by giving her tranquilizers. Because he didn't understand what was happening, he couldn't address her problem effectively, and he couldn't spare eight-year-old Gary the anguish of losing his beloved mother to a fatal overdose. However, the net this man cast for his son held. His parenting was "good enough" and strong enough, to prevent his child from plunging into hopelessness about the essential goodness of the world and of himself. If a child can continue to believe in his fundamental worth and the basic decency of other people, he will remain, at the deepest layer of the self, a healthy person. Although his emotional growth, and even his intellectual development may be blocked for a time, he will be able to advance once conditions improve.

The quality and type of parenting required to maintain a child's feeling of hope will differ according to a family's circumstance and the resilience of a particular child. Children tend to be more vulnerable at younger ages, and during those periods when, propelled by a wish for mastery as we   as a desire to please those they love, they turn to face crucial developmental challenges, such as walking, acquiring the fundamentals of speech, or adjusting to a new school. Children are also more deeply affected by a long-standing alcoholic problem, particularly if no one in the family has acknowledged or explained it, and if the adults involved regard it with an attitude of shame and fear. In general, however, you will be a good-enough parent if you are able to perceive your children's most urgent physical and emotional needs most of the time, are able to respond to those needs most of the time—at least in the sense of acknowledging their legitimacy and importance—and can fulfill them more often than not.

The concept of good-enough parenting was introduced by a British psychoanalyst named D.W. Winnicott,[1] and was discussed more recently by the late child analyst, Bruno Bettelheim[2]. It rests on the idea that the self of the child is free to unfold and develop in a natural and healthy way if parents generally orient themselves toward the child and his needs, rather than expecting the child to discern and fulfill their own needs. Naturally, as time goes on, and children mature, we expect them to take over a greater portion of their own care, and to exhibit a reasonable degree of sensitivity to the needs of the adults in the household. But when children are required, from a very young age, to preoccupy themselves with their parents' emotional needs, and continually deny their own craving for care, it is at the expense of their own individuality, emotional growth, and sense of security and well-being.

Children are necessarily dependent beings. They are unable to provide for their own physical survival, and it is only over time that they learn to muster their inner resources and utilize outside support to maintain their emotional balance. For a very extended period, your child will have to rely on you for food, shelter, and protection from abuse and exploitation. He will also need you to act as his interpreter and his adviser as he attempts to unravel the meaning of complex and significant events in his world, and as he tries to manage his emotional reactions to these events and to devise effective responses to them.

If you can accept your child's massive and inevitable need for you, and are able to convey to him that it is important to you to do your best to provide the care he needs, he will have the time, energy, and unclouded concentration he needs to tackle the intellectual and psychological tasks that will lead to emotional maturity. However, if your child feels that you resent his dependency on you, and comes to expect rejection rather than enthusiasm when he approaches you for help, he may will himself into a bogus maturity that is characterized by the appearance of self-sufficiency. Children from alcoholic homes are often superachieving family "heroes," or delinquent and hostile family "scapegoats." Whether they achieve worldly success or not, however, their attitude is typically, "I don't need you—I can take care of myself."

These children take care of themselves in a very primitive and desperate way, however. In essence, they hide themselves by denying their longing for love and care from other people. In time, they may actually "forget" that this part of themselves exists. However, the need for love will eventually make itself known, either through frequent episodes of physical illness or in periodic outbursts of depression, panic, or rage.

Feeling Safe

The principal aim of therapeutic parenting is to free children to be children and to free parents to experience and express the joy and love that is naturally a part of the parent-child relationship. In other words, the true self of a child, including his need to play and to express childish dependency, should be easily voiced, and greeted with pleasure by parents who have the energy and self-confidence to relish the parental role. In fact, your child will feel it is safe to depend on you only if you provide adequately for his physical and emotional well-being, and only if you are able to convey that it is pleasing to you to do so.

Every parent has periodic bouts of frustration with the natural order of childish dependency and adult responsibility. Times of prolonged family crisis are inevitably times of increased responsibility, and it is likely that your enthusiasm for the parental role will intermittently and progressively wane should the crisis drag on. Your behavior and attitude can remain therapeutic, however, if you are able to accept and believe that your child *must remain in a dependent position,* if you strive to *obtain whatever sense of satisfaction is possible* as you care for your child, and *secure outside help* as necessary to meet your child's most urgent needs. By the same token, you must resolve *not to punish* your child for his dependent condition. Although it is fine, and necessary at times, to tell your child that you are unable to give him something he wants or needs, it is hurtful to shame him for wanting or needing it.

STARVING FOR LOVE

The summer my mother left, I was eleven, and I was virtually my father's prisoner. I cleaned the house and baby-sat for my brothers all day long, and cooked for my father when he came home at night. Then I put my brothers to bed and collapsed myself. One day a friend from school called and invited me to a birthday party. My father freaked out when I asked if I could go. He ranted and raved and asked me how I could be so selfish and heartless to think of abandoning him and my brothers. I couldn't argue with him back then. In fact, I fainted from feeling so tired and so trapped. I still feel trapped. I still can't do anything for myself, because if I try, a voice in my head tells me I'm mean and selfish. Then I eat a pint of ice cream or a bag of cookies and throw up, just to prove how rotten I really am.

Dana—Age twenty-six

Getting Started

Your initial objective as a therapeutic parent in an alcoholic home is to gradually reclaim critical parental functions that have been ceded to the disease of alcoholism. Your principal responsibility as a parent is the psychological and physical protection of your child. However, if you are alcoholic, or have a spouse who is alcoholic, it is likely that managing the family disease has become a nearly full-time occupation—or preoccupation. If so, your child is probably occupied with learning to take care of himself. Some of the survival skills he acquires in this way will serve him well in life. However, if he spends most of his childhood under the impression that he is on his own—with no one bigger, stronger, and smarter to watch over him—he will become obsessed with the concept of self-preservation. Feeling alone, watching his back, hiding his feelings and needs since he knows they cannot be answered, hardly able to relax for fear that a fresh crisis is just ahead and waiting to overwhelm him, he will never fulfill his emotional and intellectual potential. He simply will not have the energy to devote to the matter of his own development. Therefore, you should begin your campaign to eliminate the destructive effects of alcoholism in your home by creating or re-creating a secure environment for your child.

Several crucial elements form the meshwork of a rugged and resilient emotional safety net. You will best protect your child's physical and psychological well-being by working for emotional honesty, emotional stability, and emotional responsiveness in yourself, and by supporting your child as he struggles toward these same goals. Chapters 5, 6, and 7 describe the things that you can do to establish an emotionally honest, stable, and responsive environment in which the self of a child may be both restored and fortified for a new period of growth. Chapter 8 discusses measures that parents in actively alcoholic homes may have to take to protect the physical safety of their children.

THE THERAPUTIC PARENT

- Is good enough

- Accepts her child's need to depend on her

- Preserves hope and restores emotional health by

  - Expressing love, compassion, and understanding

  - Sensing, accepting, and responding to heightened emotional needs

  - Acting as a barrier against traumatic pain

  - Ensuring physical safety and security

NOTES

1 D.W. Winnicott, *Through Paediatrics to Psycho-analysis* (New York: Basic Books, 1975.)
2 B. Bettelheim, *A Good-Enough Parent* (New York: Vintage Books, 1987.)

= 5 =

Being Emotionally Honest
With Your Children

Alcoholism, when it is untreated, diverts a substantial portion of a family's intellectual, creative, and emotional resources to the task of concealing emotional truth. Denial progresses in stages, just as alcoholism does. In the beginning it is necessary to cover up the problematic drinking. Later, members feel they must hide the effects of the drinking, which include the financial, emotional, spiritual, and physical deterioration of the family. In the end, no one in the family can tell a significant emotional truth; no one really knows one.

If you press your child to deny the anger and hurt he feels about your drinking, or that of your spouse, you are really asking him to reject or transform a critical aspect of his internal reality. He will very likely try to comply with your demand, since he loves you and wants to please and protect you. He will try not to confront you with his real needs, and will, in fact, do his best to obliterate his awareness of these needs. Over time, he will develop real difficulty in determining which parts of himself are real, and which parts have been manufactured to soothe and support you and other members of your troubled family. He will become terribly confused, and extremely frustrated. Unable to turn to you for help, full of shame over the fact that he still needs you at all, he will become highly vulnerable to a variety of emotional disorders, and will be drawn to experiences that reduce, at least temporarily, the tremendous emotional pain he is experiencing. Like so many other children from alcoholic homes, he may become depressed, chronically anxious, or withdrawn. Furthermore, he may develop severe problems with alcohol, drugs, food, sex, or money.

If you are determined to alter the unhealthy conditions in your home, you must establish an emotionally honest household. The first step toward this goal is to remove the cloak of secrecy and deception that surrounds the drinking problem itself.

Acknowledging the Alcoholism

The Recovering Alcoholic Parent

As a recovering alcoholic, you may achieve a stable sobriety, acquire extensive knowledge of your disease, construct a solid base of self-understanding, and still find self-acceptance elusive. Many people with years of sobriety, and otherwise strong programs of recovery still find it hard to look back on their years of drinking with real compassion for themselves. They *think* of alcoholism as a disease, but they *believe*, deep in their hearts, that their drinking was a moral problem and a reflection of their personal weakness. In this society, we prize self-control so highly that it is difficult for recovering alcoholics not to secretly abhor themselves for their inability to control their use of alcohol.

If you are newly sober, it may be especially hard for you to take responsibility for your problematic drinking without also condemning yourself for the trouble it has caused you and your family. Deep feelings of shame and regret make it hard to tell children the truth behind the family's struggles. You may find that you are sorely tempted to turn your back on the troubled past, to concentrate intently on the future, and to set about implementing your resolution to change yourself and your relationship with your spouse and child.

Unfortunately, your child will not be able to break with the past until he fully grasps its meaning. If you ignore or deny what has happened as a result of your drinking, you will temporarily avoid a painful confrontation with your feelings of shame and self-doubt. However, your youngster will remain alone with his massive emotional confusion. He will also be alone with his own feeling of overwhelming responsibility for the family's suffering. Like other children in alcoholic families, yours almost certainly blames himself for your distress, and that of your spouse. He imagines that he is the cause of inconsistencies and instances of abuse and neglect in your past behavior. Whereas he will certainly be heartened by your sobriety and your efforts to build a stronger and healthier relationship with him, unless you help him to understand your drinking and its impact on the family, he will continue to be frightened by his memories of the past and he will continue to believe that he was the source of your suffering.

You have a great deal of power to release your child from his confusion and feelings of shame. He looks to you for an understanding of the crucial events in his life, and he wants, more than anything else, to feel that you regard him as valuable, and lovable. When you tell him that you are a recovering alcoholic, and explain how your drinking has affected you and your relationship with your family, your honesty will help to restore your child's emotional integrity and his self-regard.

First of all, you will be placing your alcoholism at the center of events that have plagued your family. This will relieve your child of the burden of responsibility he feels for the bad things that have happened. It also helps him to understand why he has been feeling so bad. Once he understands that there are good reasons for the pain he is feeling, he will have less shame about feeling it, and less reason to compromise his hold on reality by denying it. Second, by acknowledging your alcoholism and its effects, you will demonstrate to your child that you are willing to accept the pain that comes with telling the truth if it will support his sense of well-being. He will sense that bringing the alcoholism to light is a difficult, frightening step for you, and he will sense that you are doing it for him. Your child will experience your effort as an act of love. He will feel far less alone, and he will be fortified by your courage, and your caring. Some of the information you may wish to give to your child, as you discuss your alcoholism, is presented in the section of this chapter that describes family meetings.

The Recovering Codependent Parent

Very often, the sober parent must take the lead in creating an atmosphere of emotional honesty in the alcoholic family. The first step in this process is a monumental one. It is to be honest with yourself, then with your spouse, and then with your child about what has likely become the central fact of life in your home: the alcoholic's drinking.

The alcoholism *must* be acknowledged, but you, like many other spouses of alcoholics, may be highly reluctant to take this step. Perhaps you feel paralyzed by self-doubt. You sense that something is terribly wrong at home. In your heart, you blame your spouse's drinking for the breakdown of your family. However, if you have little information about the disease and how it is diagnosed, you will be vulnerable to her defensive denial of the problem and to her attempts to displace responsibility by accusing you of being "crazy" and a constant nag. Her accusations will join with your confusion and ignorance to kindle a deep uncertainty about the real cause of the trouble at home. This uncertainty will hinder you from taking action to help yourself and your family.

Once you are armed with facts, however, you will be in a much better position to fend off the alcoholic's denial, which is nothing more than a prominent and universal symptom of the disease she is suffering. An addictions specialist (see chapter 10) can describe the symptoms of the disease and its progression, and help you to determine whether or not your spouse is drinking alcoholically. A great deal of literature is also available at Al-Anon meetings or at open meetings of Alcoholics Anonymous. Additional helpful readings are listed in the Suggested Reading section of this book.

Once you reach the conclusion that your spouse is drinking alcoholically, there is another imposing task before you. Unless you feel that you would place yourself in physical danger to do so, you must face your spouse with your belief that she is an alcoholic. This is important because your goal is, once again, to reclaim territory that has been invaded and corrupted by the alcoholism. As long as you feel that you must disguise and conceal your true reactions to her and to her behavior, you will feel cornered and cowed by her disease. This will have a profound effect on your self-respect, as well as on your emotional stability. It will, therefore, impair your ability to lead your children to higher and safer emotional ground.

Your ability to confront your spouse with the truth about what is happening to her, and to you and your children, *may* influence her to enter treatment. Of course, you and your children can move forward whether or not the alcoholic continues to drink. However, unless you have already decided to end your marriage, you undoubtedly are hoping and praying for her recovery. You cannot force your spouse to stop drinking. However, you can make your home a healthier place, and increase the odds that she will seek treatment if you are honest with her now.

Most alcoholics, especially those who have been drinking in a compulsive fashion for many years, require intensive treatment to achieve stable sobriety. Unfortunately, their massive denial prevents them from acknowledging their problem and the need for this treatment. Some eventually enter a program when they experience some sort of personal disaster, such as the breakup of a marriage, that represents "bottom" for them and shatters their denial. It is agonizing to wait for this final crisis, and many alcoholics and their families suffer immense and irreversible damage before they seek treatment. It is possible, however, to create a crisis that will drive an alcoholic into treatment, by confronting her with testimonial evidence of the damage her drinking has caused. This technique is called an "intervention." It was pioneered by Vernon Johnson[1], of the Johnson Institute in Minneapolis. It has been used to move thousands of alcoholics into treatment. Although it can be performed at any stage of the disease, it is desirable to confront your alcoholic as early as possible in his drinking career, before your family incurs terrible losses. The technique of intervention is summarized in Appendix I.

Whether or not you decide to conduct an intervention for your alcoholic spouse, you must make the subject of her drinking a topic for open family discussion. Your children are unlikely to speak freely about the drinking and the way it hurts them, unless you can do it, first with your spouse and then with them. Once you have talked to your spouse, you can meet with your children to describe your new understanding of what is troubling the family, and to present any plans that have taken shape as a result of an intervention.

The Family Meeting

When you first approach your children about the topic of alcoholism, and as you pursue a program of family recovery, you should begin to hold formal family meetings. These meetings will help to convince your children that you are serious about taking a new approach to family life. These meetings will mark, clearly the beginning of a new era of candor about alcoholism and any other events or interactions that are troubling to family members. Formulating agendas for these meetings is also important. You don't need to adhere rigidly to your agenda, and you should keep it short, since these meetings are but one aspect of your campaign to open the family emotionally. On the other hand, if you (and your spouse and children) sit down and formulate a list of topics that you feel are important to discuss, it will help you to identify the family's most urgent psychological and emotional needs. You will also have a better sense of how you want to use your time in the meeting.

Whereas different families in different situations will have different goals for this first meeting, it is important to provide children with basic information about alcoholism and its typical effects on the family as soon as possible. It is also important to begin to teach children some of the emotional skills that facilitate recovery from familial alcoholism. This chapter (and chapters 1 and 2) contain fundamental information about alcoholism and recovery that you may wish to review as you develop the agenda for the first meeting, and as you begin to think about future family conferences. However, you should plan to tackle only one or two important topics in your first family meeting, and you should only expect to begin work on these topics.

Above all, children must understand that alcoholism is a family problem. Children's recovery from the effects of parental alcoholism depends on their ability to acknowledge and identify these effects. You can help them with this process by presenting the alcoholism as a dilemma the entire family faces, rather than as a problem that rests solely with their drinking parent. However, you should be careful to explain, time and again, what this means. Clearly, it does *not* mean that they or their sober parent caused the compulsive drinking, or that anyone but the drinker has the power to stop it. It does mean that everyone in the family has been changed by the fact of the drinking, and that everyone must acknowledge and discuss these changes, for the sake of their own health and that of the family as well.

Your children should be introduced to the disease model of alcoholism as soon as a medical diagnosis of alcoholism is made, or shortly after a sober parent has become convinced that her spouse is drinking alcoholically. As we have seen, children take enormous and undue responsibility for a parent's drinking. The most effective way to relieve them of this burden is to help them understand that alcoholic drinkers are ill. The disease perspective presented in chapter 2 has five central theses. First, although alcoholism may be aggravated by emotional and psychological conflicts, most alcoholics have a constitutional predisposition to compulsive drinking. Second, alcoholism is a condition that usually gets worse over time. Third, it is an incurable disease, but may be brought under control through total abstinence from alcohol. Fourth, alcoholism is a disease characterized by relapse.

Most people "slip" on their way to a stable sobriety, and some slip badly, creating real trouble for themselves and their families. This does not mean that treatment has failed, or that everything that was achieved during the sober period has been destroyed. It only means that the program for recovery must be altered in some way to address the problems that precipitated a new round of drinking. Finally, alcoholism is never a result of family problems. On the contrary, alcoholism produces a host of severe family problems.

Even if your children have been exposed to these five ideas already, it is a good idea to present them again at an early point in the initial family conference and to emphasize the fact that no one is responsible for causing an alcoholic to drink. Again, you should go on to explain that although a family can do many things to support an alcoholic's recovery, once she has stopped drinking, an alcoholic needs help from people outside the family to actually stop.

EDUCATING CHILDREN ABOUT ALCOHOLISM

- Alcoholism is a disease

    It is a condition of suffering
    It usually has a genetic component

- Alcoholism is a family disease

    Everyone is affected by the drinking
    But no one caused the drinking and
    Only the drinker can take steps to stop it

- Alcoholism is a chronic disease

  It usually gets worse if it is not treated

- Alcoholism cannot be cured

  It may be controlled through abstinence

- Alcoholism is a relapsing condition

- Alcoholism is not caused by family problems or an "addictive personality"

  But it does cause many personal and family problems

The next two sections offer suggestions about preparing for and conducting a program of regular family meetings. The suggestions for recovering alcoholic parents concern the importance of identifying and overcoming resistances to greater emotional intimacy with your children. The section for recovering codependent parents describes ways in which you and your children can begin to address the issues that have been troubling you and your children, but have seemed too sensitive to discuss openly. All readers should peruse both sections. There is much material in each section of common interest.

The Recovering Alcoholic Parent: Getting Ready for Family Meetings

During the first year of your recovery, and even afterward, your professional helpers and your peers in Alcoholics Anonymous will be working to topple the wall of denial that you built while you were drinking. This wall has shielded you from many disturbing truths about your life, including the extent of your drinking problem and its effects on you and your family.

Now that you are sober, you and your loved ones may expect that you will see yourself and your drinking in a clear light, and easily understand and acknowledge your role in the family's struggle. In fact, a deep understanding of these problems is quite difficult to achieve and develops only gradually. It will be some time before you are ready to complete a meaningful and comprehensive "moral inventory," which is the fourth step in the Twelve-Step Program of recovery prescribed by Alcoholics Anonymous. It is usually wise to postpone extensive self-analysis until your sobriety is stable and your recovery has progressed to a point at which you view yourself, and your past with genuine compassion. Otherwise, your inventory can become a demoralizing catalog of perceived failures, rather than the balanced accounting of strengths, achievements, mistakes, and shortcomings that it is intended to be.

However, it is important, as noted previously, to directly acknowledge the fact of your alcoholism to your children, and to explain, time and again, that your sobriety and other aspects of your recovery always were and always will be your responsibility. It is also important that you *begin* to share other parts of your emotional life with your children in a much deeper way than you were able to do when you were drinking. Emotional honesty means telling the truth about what you do and why you do it. It also means revealing who you truly are, what you truly believe and feel.

Family meetings provide a superb forum for self-revelation and a frank exchange of feelings. However, opening yourself emotionally to your children will probably feel like a risky proposition in the beginning. Denial and repression have fostered the progress of your disease, it is true. However, they have also shielded you, to some extent, from painful feelings that have threatened to destroy your sense of self worth. If you were abused or neglected as a child, you probably relied heavily on these defenses even then, as a means of preserving some measure of hope about life and the possibility of finding kindness and care in the world. It is very hard, and, in fact, should be very hard, to relinquish methods and tools that have served your psychological survival, even though you understand that they are now hindering your psychological and emotional growth. Therefore, you must expect to change slowly. You must, as they say in Alcoholics Anonymous, seek "progress, not perfection."

Because you are naturally reluctant to expose your own feelings and may also fear confronting intense emotions that your family is experiencing, and because your spouse and children have also learned to hide what they're really feeling and thinking, it is unlikely that honest, intimate emotional exchanges will occur spontaneously in your family meetings. You will have to work hard to achieve a more honest posture with one another. Your children will look to you and your spouse for guidance and an understanding of the real purposes of the family meeting. They will wonder if you truly intend to establish an atmosphere of emotional honesty in your home, or if you are still secretly dedicated to denying, burying, or crushing any truth that hurts. Like the soldier hiding in a cave, who refuses to trust the news of an armistice, your children will wait for solid proof of your intentions. It must come in the form of your own willingness to expose your tender, vulnerable self—your hopes, your wounds, your need for love. However, if you are now to reveal the part of yourself that you have been dedicated to concealing, you will have to come to firm grips with your resistances to emotional intimacy.

Identifying Resistances to Emotional Intimacy. Although you may truly long for open and honest emotional communication with your family, your fear of disappointing them or being hurt by them may lead youto create formidable obstacles to this kind of closeness. These obstacles may be of a practical nature, involving your physical unavailability for emotional contact, or they may entail mixed messages that you give your family about your desire for real intimacy with them. You will be taking an important step toward honesty and openness with your family if you will be frank with yourself as you consider the following questions:

- Am I home and emotionally accessible at times when my spouse and children are able to spend time relaxing and talking with me?
  - Am I present for important family gatherings? Do I take at least one meal a day with the family? Do I initiate and attend important family outings? Do I get to every family meeting, and get there on time?
  - Am I making my family my first priority right now? Or am I placing work first? If I'm very preoccupied with work right now, is this a necessity? Could I be avoiding facing certain feelings in myself and in my loved ones?
  - Do I signal my willingness to talk when I'm with my family? Do I turn off the television, put down the paper, and ask them how they're feeling?
- Am I trying to help my children know the real me?
  - Have I told them about my illness?
  - Have I described what I will do to get better?
  - Do I share significant experiences (highs and lows) in a way my children can understand?
  - When I talk about events that are important to me, do I tell my children how I feel about these events, and why?
  - Do I tell my children about mistakes I've made, with them and with other people?
  - Have I told my children about the events in my life that have made me who I am? Do I explain how I felt when these things happened, and how I feel about them now?
  - Do I tell my children, directly, when I feel angry at them? When I feel loving toward them? When I want their help with something?

- Am I trying to encourage my children to reveal their real feelings?
  - Do I ask them to tell me how they feel?
  - Do I allow them to tell me how they feel about me, even when they're angry or disappointed with me? Can I listen to their feelings of hurt and frustration without punishing them—condemning their behavior and attitude or pulling away and freezing them out?

None of us is an open book to our children, or to anyone else for that matter. However, if you find that you are frequently away from your family, or that you are preoccupied with business when you are at home; if you discuss events with your family without telling them your reactions to these events, and even tell yourself that events in your life are too trivial, or too disturbing to discuss with children; if you observe yourself attacking or withdrawing from your children when they reveal their own emotional lives to you, it is very likely that you are actively avoiding and deflecting opportunities for an emotional exchange with your children. Although you may tell your children that you want to be closer to them, they will feel you fleeing from such closeness, and they will tell themselves that you are too frightened or too disinterested to make good on your conscious intentions. They will probably secretly believe that you would share yourself more freely if *they* were only smarter, or better behaved, or more lovable. At any rate, they will try to protect themselves from further disappointment by evading intimacy in the same ways that you do.

Overcoming Your Fears of Emotional Intimacy. If you are to conquer your fear of revealing yourself to your children, you will have to spend some time exploring the nature of your fear, and you will also have to practice talking to other people about yourself.

Many people find that it is easier (though not easy), to begin talking about themselves and their feelings to a journal that remains private, at least for a time. Keeping a journal of day-to-day events, and the feelings they arouse, can help you to become more attuned to your own inner life. This could be the first step to richer communication with other people, including your children. You can use your journal to practice making "I" statements, describing not just particular events, but your own complex reactions to these events. The more uncomfortable you are with your feelings, and the more you tend to worry about others' reactions to you, the more tempted you will feel to concentrate on the actions of others when your write in your journal. You can correct this tendency to focus outside yourself by making a conscious effort to start sentences with phrases like, "I think, I believe," and "I feel." "I" statements force you to look inside for information about experiences, and help you to understand and acknowledge your own role in shaping them.

Keeping a journal will help you to a deeper understanding of yourself and your emotional life, but outside stimulation and support are also important when you are trying to figure out just who you are without alcohol and other drugs. If you attend some speaker's meetings through Alcoholics Anonymous, you will be able to observe other people in the act of examining their lives, and this may help you to think about aspects of your own experience that you have been reluctant to examine. There is no pressure at all to share at a speaker's meeting, so you will be able to devote your energy to listening to the speaker's story and the ways in which it does, or does not, jibe with your own. Later, you can use your journal to record important memories and feelings that were stirred at the meeting.

When you feel more practiced at talking to yourself about yourself, and are on friendlier terms with your own "emotional" self, your next step should be to try and talk to someone outside your family whom you have begun to trust, and whom you know to be knowledgeable about addiction and recovery. It is important to find a calm and nonjudgmental listener who understands and supports your immediate aims. At this point you are not evaluating your character and you are not pursuing monumental life changes. Rather, you are trying to describe your feelings in a simple and straightforward way. Your listener will best help by listening silently, or by asking you to give examples when you say something she doesn't understand.

If it feels very frightening to speak about drinking, or recovery right now, don't force yourself. Choose a more comfortable topic—one that has some personal meaning for you but doesn't arouse such terrible anxiety or shame that you feel compelled to run away. It may be easier to talk about your work for example, if you feel that you're in pretty good shape there. You can begin by describing things that you feel good about, and, as you grow more comfortable, you can share any feelings of pressure or anxiety that you are experiencing. If you meet with your listener several times, you will have time to develop a feeling of trust in her ability to listen without judging you, and you will eventually be able to discuss more sensitive topics with her.

When you do feel able to speak about experiences that relate directly to drinking and to recovery, you will also be ready to identify some of the specific fears that are blocking your efforts to speak honestly and openly with your family. Once again, it may be helpful to write about your fears before you try to express them to your outside, objective listener. Try to picture yourself at a family meeting with your spouse and children. Imagine that you are saying to them, "I am an alcoholic. I think we should talk with each other about what that means." What feelings are you aware of as you imagine saying these words? What do you imagine your spouse is feeling? How do you suppose your children would react? Record your scarier imaginings in your journal, along with any comforting images that come to mind.

Now schedule another appointment with a nonjudgmental listener. At this point, it will be most helpful if you can talk to another recovering addict or alcoholic who has a stable sobriety and a solid program in AA. First, describe your worst fears about sharing yourself more openly with your family. Read from your journal if you become anxious or confused and can't find the words to express your fears. Also, ask your colleague about the emotional obstacles she encountered as she moved toward a more honest and self-revealing posture with her family. What were her great fears, and how did she master them? Did any of her personal nightmares about telling the truth come to pass? If so, how did she cope when her family behaved badly in the face of her revelations?

By this time you should have a somewhat clearer understanding of the fears that are preventing you from becoming closer to your children emotionally. Most recovering people struggle with three principal fears when they first try to share feelings about themselves and their illness. First of all, they are terrified that when they acknowledge the past, the pain they have felt and caused, they will be overwhelmed by feelings of shame and self-disgust. Second, they fear that any frank discussion of conflict in the family will lead inevitably to an explosive confrontation about the drinking and its destructive effects on the family. Alcoholics in early recovery are struggling to preserve a sense of hope about life and the possibility of feeling valuable and beloved once again. Most understand, at some level, that if their own dark feelings about themselves are suddenly and powerfully released, their sense of worth may be completely destroyed. Finally, many alcoholics in the initial stages of recovery are afraid that if everyone's hurt about the drinking is brought to the surface, the *family* may be destroyed, and they may be left totally alone.

There is a good chance that your children will respond to your honesty with expressions of relief and pride about your courageous decision to change your life and your relationship with them. But conflict is a normal aspect of family life, and if you succeed in opening and broadening the channels of communication with your children, they will sometimes feel and directly express rage toward you. Even if your children are usually supportive and loving, you will have to confront your own shame about the past. Shameful feelings are bound to arise as you look back, but you will have to look back in order to thoroughly accept your alcoholism and work toward real change in your life. Here are some suggestions for managing your pain and preserving your self-esteem as you turn to face the truth and begin to reveal it to your children:

- Surround yourself with support and opportunities for positive interactions with others.

    There will probably be times when you resent the many hours you devote to recovery activities. However, your life was more or less consumed by drinking (and dealing with the effects of drinking) before, and it will have to be dominated by active recovery efforts for awhile. Affirming and inspiring interactions with others are essential if you are to manage your shame and grief about the past. The most powerful recovery strategies combine AA attendance with some other form of direct emotional support (e.g., individual or group counseling with a recovery focus.)

- Remind yourself that your goal is to manage conflict with yourself and others, not avoid it.

    Painful emotions and experiences are normal in recovery. Moreover, they are a necessary part of our humanity. We get into more trouble by resisting emotional pain than we do by feeling it, expressing it honestly to those we love and trust, and working with them toward a resolution of it.

- Recognize that your children are also struggling with feelings of shame and worthlessness.

    If your children lash out in cruel and destructive ways, it is probably because they feel responsible for the family's pain. No one can endure this kind of terrible shame without complaint. If your children are relatively isolated from outside support, they will "manage" their burden of shame by becoming ill or by periodically dumping it onto you or some other vulnerable person(s). Chapter 6, on emotional stability, describes ways of helping your children to express their anger and hurt in an honest and constructive way. Some children seem compelled to continue acting out their distress. Chapter 10 discusses how to seek professional help for children who cannot stop hurting themselves and others.

- Make certain that members of your family learn how to express positive feelings for one another.

    One recovering father was shocked to learn, during a family therapy session, that his adult son wasn't certain of his father's feelings for him. "You've never said that you loved me," the son observed.

    "But you *must* know that," the father cried, "Surely I've shown you, even if I haven't said it."

    "I don't really know it," the son said, as tears filled his eyes. "I've never been sure. I keep trying to understand what it means that you don't say it. I've always been afraid that there's something about me that you just can't love."

The ability to express love and support for one another is an essential component of emotional honesty, for it inspires hope in family members.

- Reserve a time, at the beginning and the end of each family meeting, for members to exchange positive feelings about each other. If your children can't share positive observations or loving feelings at first, make sure that you and your spouse, at least, have an affirming word or two for each person at the meeting.
- Create opportunities for you and your children to play together. Periods of conflict and pain are easier to weather when there is a solid core of good feelings between parent and child. It takes time and focused effort to build, or rebuild this core. Take the time to enjoy recreational activities with your children. Play time should be devoted to play. Try to avoid work-related distractions.
- Remember to say, "I love you."

BREAKING THE ICE

My daughter was eight, and my son was five when I stopped drinking. It literally took years for me to tell them the whole truth about my drinking. It was a long time before I could even use the word, "alcoholic." I was just too ashamed. But since I was a single parent, I had to take my kids with me to AA meetings. They liked the cookies and the soft drinks, but they also listened, and they met a lot of people who were recovering from a drinking problem and who were farther along than I was. Those people were able to say things about alcoholism that I just couldn't say at that time, and it helped us to start talking.

Rusty—Age fifty-two

The Recovering Codependent Parent: Conducting Family Meetings

If you are living with an actively alcoholic spouse, you must struggle daily with your own fear and despair, as well as that of your children. Over time, you will probably come to feel that it is your deepest wish, and your foremost responsibility, to quell the turbulent feelings that torment your family. Many spouses of alcoholics suppress and deny their own anger and disappointment and believe that they are helping their children when they teach them to bury their unhappy feelings as well.

Unfortunately, a child's inner torment only increases when it is suppressed, and the effort required to keep it buried eventually breeds all manner of psychological maladies, including depressive illness, panic disorders, and addictive problems. Children must have an outlet for the pain they feel about a parent's drinking. Most of all, they need to know that this pain matters to you, that you can hear it and remain strong and loving, and that you will comfort them. Although it will hurt you to hear that your children have been hurt, you must try to welcome their anger and their sadness even when it is directed toward you. Try to remember that your children's ability to speak with you about their anger and pain is evidence of their underlying belief in your strength, and the resilience of the bond between you. In fact, your greatest assurance that you have become a therapeutic parent will be your children's willingness to expose their hurt to you and to bring their conflicts with you and your spouse into the open.

At some point, either in the first meeting, or at a later family gathering, you will want to initiate what should become an ongoing exchange of feelings about the drinking, and the process of recovery. Children often have difficulty labeling and discussing emotions, even when they feel them strongly. You can help your children to engage more fully in this kind of discussion by identifying the kinds of feelings that children and grown-ups typically have in alcoholic families. You will naturally want to adjust your vocabulary to your children's level of understanding and their ability to label and express feelings. Older, fairly articulate children may catch on quickly and begin to volunteer some of their reactions if you simply suggest that children in alcoholic families often feel angry, frightened, and disappointed about the drinking and fighting in their homes. Even preschoolers can get the idea if you use fairly broad emotional categories and speak of very recent events they witnessed and that obviously upset them.

For example, one mother who had grown up in an extremely dysfunctional family, and who was struggling with a depression of her own, worried about the effects that her fluctuations in mood had on her four-year-old daughter. This woman had many days when she was preoccupied with her own feelings of inadequacy and entrapment. When she felt bad, she could not gratify her child's pleas for attention and play. The mother began to notice that when she withdrew, her child would often retreat into a sad and passive fog of her own, This particular young woman had always blamed herself for her mother's unpredictable and terrifying rage, which was never explained to her. She was afraid that her daughter was assuming a similar burden of shameful responsibility, and so, she tried to tell the child the truth.

On one particularly difficult occasion, she said to her child, "I'm having a bad day today. I'm thinking of things that happened to me when I was little that made me feel very sad."

Her daughter replied, "And things that scared you?" "Yes, things that scared me," the mother said.

This was enough to lift the child's spirits. Some days later, the daughter witnessed an argument between her parents and was obviously downcast afterward. The mother initiated another exchange.

This time, the mother said, "I got really angry at Daddy."

The little girl asked, "Did you want to hit him?"

Mother answered, "Yes, I feel like that sometimes, but I don't do it."

"Do you ever feel mad enough to kill someone?" the child asked.

"Yes," the mother replied, "I do. But if I talk about why I'm angry, that feeling goes away." Then the mother asked, "Do you ever feel mad enough to kill someone?"

At this point, the daughter explained that she often felt this way about her baby-sitter. As the conversation continued, it became clear that the baby-sitter was preoccupied with the needs of the infant in the home, and that the older child was experiencing strong feelings of hurt and resentment on this account.

This mother had always felt ashamed of her depression and her temper, and had tried for a long time to suppress and conceal her emotional conflicts. But she understood that her daughter was suffering because of this denial. The mother's straightforward, simple accounting of her emotional experience on these two occasions relieved her child of the fear that she might be the object of the frightening emotions in the air, and encouraged her to open up about a troubling problem in her own life.

EMOTIONAL HONESTY AND SHARING FEELINGS: PAUL'S FAMILY

Paul was the father of two preteenage sons. He was filled with grief over his alcoholic wife's abandonment of him and his boys. He believed, however, that his children would be shattered if they learned of his sadness. He affected an attitude of brash self-confidence with them, and avoided occasions and discussions that might remind him, or them, of the family's great loss. The boys naturally emulated their father's example and soon no one dared mention mother, let alone grieve for her.

In time, this little family began to experience great conflict over issues of chores and money. They were not strained financially. The family employed a housekeeper, and the boys had an abundance of material possessions. Still, both children protested fiercely when asked to perform minor household duties, and both nagged their father constantly for toys and outings. If Paul refused their requests, they denounced him as a cruel, withholding tyrant. He could not abide their disappointment, and usually met whatever demand the boys were pressing at the moment, but he felt exploited by his sons. He remarked to a friend that it seemed as though he had lost his entire family in the short and shocking space of a single year.

A family counselor suggested to this young father that, in one way or another, he and his sons were always talking with one another about frustrated longings. The counselor wondered if the boys' constant demands for more things and greater pleasures might reflect suppressed grief for their absent mother. The counselor proposed to Paul that the denial of loss would be more damaging to his sons than the direct experience of it. She encouraged him to speak with them, as much as he could, about his own sadness.

A few days later, Paul accompanied Jay, his ten-year-old, on a school outing. Most of the other parental escorts were mothers, and Paul was acutely aware of the somber demeanor his son exhibited throughout the day. Afterwards, as they drove home together, Paul said to Jay, " I really miss Mom sometimes." Tears came to Jay's eyes immediately, but he said nothing. "I know you and Doug miss her, too," Paul continued. "It's okay to tell me that." Jay could only cry quietly as his father drove on. It was some time before this family spoke openly with one another about the tragedy they had experienced. But the process of sharing their grief began with Paul's modest, yet powerful, attempt to communicate a portion of his own pain, and his explicit invitation to Jay to respond in kind.

Another thing that a recovering codependent parent can do to help children to examine and express their feelings is to share his own reactions to the alcoholic's drinking and how it has affected the family. You may describe how frightened you are that your spouse will have an accident while under the influence, or how angry you feel when she falls asleep after dinner, instead of spending time with you and the children. You may worry that you sound like a chronic complainer as you say these things, or that your children will think you want their sympathy or caretaking. It's actually a good idea to worry about this, because you don't want to present yourself to your children as a victim. Your goal is to help your children identify serious problems in the family, so that the family can work together toward the resolution of these problems. Sharing feelings is a way of identifying problem areas, and it necessarily entails the airing of serious complaints. However, the aim is not to condemn the drinker, or to break into warring camps. It is to speak honestly about what has gone wrong, identify individual and family needs, and set about righting things.

Although it is important to get feelings about the drinking on the table as soon as possible, it will greatly enlarge your children's emotional world and increase their trust in you, if you can also describe your feelings about the role you have assumed in the family. You will certainly want to enumerate the constructive things you feel you've accomplished and assure your children that they can continue to count on you for these things. But it is also important to be as honest as you can be about mistakes you have made. This is hard to do, but bear in mind that in most cases you will be speaking with your children about things they already know, and to which they have already had powerful reactions, even though these reactions may be suppressed and denied.

For example, you, like hundreds of thousands of other codependent spouses, may have enabled your alcoholic's drinking in a number of ways. You may have covered for her with family, friends, and employers by making excuses for her lapses. Perhaps you let her drive when you knew she was too drunk to do so safely. Or maybe you avoided a scene by giving her liquor or accompanying her to a bar. Your children will feel safer with you if they know that you understand that these things were mistakes, and if you state your intention to approach your spouse's drinking differently from now on.

Once you have described the kind of feelings people in alcoholic families commonly experience, and after you have shared some of your own feelings, you can invite your children to express some of their reactions. They might share feelings about the drinking, or about your behavior, or they might express thoughts about other aspects of family life.

Children should not be allowed to attack you physically or be verbally abusive while expressing their feelings. They should be given complete permission to cry with you, however, and should be allowed to tell you that they feel angry or unloving toward you. This is bound to hurt when it happens, but all children feel such things at times, and children in alcoholic families have good reason to feel sad and hateful much of the time. The material in chapter 7 concerning emotional responsiveness should help you to respond to intense feelings that your children express.

It is not important, at this time, to answer any charges of unfairness that your children make. Nor is it a good idea, right now, to explain or defend any behavior that they dislike in you or your spouse. It is important to encourage their honesty by listening to what they say, and by reminding them frequently that they have a right to feel bad. When your children come to believe that their most powerful negative feelings can be expressed directly to you, and that these feelings will be considered and soothed by you, they will, in most cases, move past their anger and disappointment. You will ultimately find that the bond of love between you and your children has been strengthened by your willingness to face the conflict between you.

The Nuts and Bolts of the Family Meeting

A program of regularly scheduled family meetings will help you and your children take the first, tentative steps toward emotional honesty with one another. Your aim is to create an atmosphere in which everyone's unhappiness, as well as everyone's joy, may be expressed, acknowledged, and understood. This end will only be achieved over time and with sustained effort.

A weekly meeting of all family members provides an opportunity for each individual to express a range of feelings about himself or the family. Some families require each member to share at least one positive and one negative experience or observation during each meeting. They also rotate responsibility for the conduct of the meetings, with a different family member assuming the chair each week or each month. It is good to keep other ground rules to a minimum.

Some problems or conflicts that are raised will be too complex to resolve in one meeting, but if more information or more time for discussion is needed, the group should set a definite date when the matter will be reopened and reconsidered. Most families who institute a regular meeting time do meet once each week. Since all members are expected to attend every meeting, it is a good idea to take some care when selecting a regular time for these conferences.

A SMALL FAMILY MEETING

Family meetings can be tailored to suit your family's unique needs. A special format may help your group to share in a more intimate way. Some most unusual meetings were held by a co-alcoholic mother and daughter, who were being seen in psychotherapy together. The daughter, Kari, was eleven years old, and had been skipping school frequently. A teacher who caught her with drug paraphernalia referred her for treatment, and Kari's mother agreed to attend the therapy sessions with her daughter on the condition that the father not be involved. It turned out that the father was alcoholic, and that one way in which Kari's mother tried to "manage" his drinking was by shielding him from family problems.

Communication between Kari and her mother was in a shambles. Driven by an intense fear that Kari would become deeply involved with alcohol and drugs, the mother constantly interrogated her daughter about friends and activities that might have occasioned drug use. Kari had withdrawn from her mother under the pressure of this continual grilling, and volunteered little if any meaningful information about her inner world, or even her day-to-day experiences. The therapist felt that Kari's behavior problems reflected tension that mother and daughter felt,but could not discuss, about the father's drinking. She also thought that Kari's mother was dissembling about the real source of her anxiety, which was the husband's drinking. The therapist believed that Kari would continue to conceal her true feelings as long as her mother was doing so.

Because Kari's mother denied the seriousness of her husband's drinking problem, and refused to invite him to family therapy, the issue of familial alcoholism could not be thoroughly addressed. However, the therapist hoped that she could strengthen the relationship between the mother and daughter, allowing the little girl to confide in her mother a bit more, and thereby relieving some of the internal strain the child was experiencing.

The therapist tried to restructure the pattern of communication between Kari and her mother, and, at the same time, tried to help Kari's mother to focus on, and clarify her own internal experience, so that she could be more honest and direct about it with Kari. She directed the mother to hold twice-weekly meetings with Kari, but to refrain from asking Kari any questions at all during these meetings. In fact, the mother was to use the time in the meetings to tell Kari stories about her own experiences as a preteenager. Kari was permitted to ask her mother questions, or to make any comment about her mother's stories, or her own experiences, that she cared to make. Of course, the therapist did other things to encourage and support change in this relationship. In particular, she gave mother and daughter information about the effects of alcoholism on codependent family members. But this format for the family meeting worked very well for them. When they practiced the "no questions asked" program in therapy sessions, Kari immediately became more involved with her mother, making eye contact with her, and even leaning forward in her chair to hear the stories about her mother's struggles with self-consciousness, peer pressure, and academic anxiety. Kari did ask her mother questions as the weeks went on, and began to open up about her own distress. After these two became fairly comfortable talking with one another, and with the therapist, about painful events and feelings, the mother agreed that the father could be invited to attend several sessions in order to work on solutions to Kari's school problems. These problems were handled successfully in family therapy and Kari was eventually excused from attending psychotherapy. Her father and mother undertook couples work together where they began to directly address the problem of her father's drinking.

An alcoholic parent in recovery may attend family meetings as soon as she completes alcohol rehabilitation. In fact, most inpatient rehabilitation programs require family counseling as a part of treatment, and this is a good way to get a program of regular family conferences off to a flying start. Even if ongoing family counseling is occurring as a part of the recovering drinker's aftercare, regular meetings at home are helpful to most recovering families as a means to practice and master the emotional, interpersonal, and problem-solving skills they are developing in counseling. Your therapist should, of course, be consulted about the structure and timing of these meetings.

An actively alcoholic spouse is more difficult to include as a regular member of the family meeting. As her disease progresses, it becomes increasingly difficult, and increasingly unwise, to count on her to keep appointments or to manage conflict in a constructive fashion. However, you can invite a drinking spouse to attend after conducting one or two successful meetings with your children. If she comes to the meeting, the group can review the ground rules it has set and ask if she would like to add to or amend any of them. If her drinking causes her to miss or disrupt any family meetings, it is best to meet without her until she is in recovery.

You should protect this time with your children. Once again, alcoholic drinking is often allowed to control nearly every aspect of family functioning. The behavior and thoughts of each member are dominated by the idea of managing, defending, or concealing the family problem. You and your children must interrupt this miserable and futile cycle by beginning to shelter significant aspects of family life from the effects of the disease. In other words, certain parts of the show really must go on, no matter what. Your family meeting time, which is devoted to the discovery and expression of the emotional truth about your lives together, should be inviolable.

It is helpful at the end of each meeting to ask each member to think about the next steps he or she will take to further the process of recovery. You can help your children to become more active in their pursuit of recovery by reviewing the problem areas they have talked about during the meeting and then asking them to identify specific goals they hope to accomplish by the next meeting. For example, an older child might decide to attend an Alateen meeting during the coming week. He can consider the problem of transportation before this meeting breaks up, making arrangements for a ride with you or with a brother or sister who drives. A younger child is not able to think ahead in this fashion, but if you sense that your toddler or preschooler is troubled, or that there is increased tension between you as a result of your preoccupation with family problems, this is a time when you can brainstorm with the family about ways to increase his sense of well-being. For example, you might be able to set up a special time for him to be alone with you, for a story and a cuddle, if the older children can agree to clear away and wash the dinner dishes. Even though a small child can't participate fully in the attempt to solve problems that involve him, he will certainly understand that the family is thinking and talking about him and how he feels. This is restorative because it reassures him that he is important to everyone, and that they remember his needs even when they have big problems of their own.

If each member of the family develops an "action plan" for the week, the group is more likely to feel that they have closed the meeting on a hopeful note. Even if some members simply agree to think more about the issues they raised, and to return for another round of discussions on these matters next week, it will feel like you're working on things, and this will be encouraging to everyone. At the end of the first meeting, at least, it will also help if you remind your children that many families suffer from the disease of alcoholism, and that many families recover. You can also talk with your children about the positive changes they have accomplished as a result of their attempts to deal with the alcoholism. Keep in mind that any crisis that we face in life has the power to strengthen us, especially if we confront it at a time when our internal resources and our external support systems are in relatively good working order. Even when optimal conditions do not prevail, many children from alcoholic families emerge from this experience with toughness, determination, insight, and compassion for the suffering of others, as well as a strong instinct for survival. Often, these children are unable to sense their admirable qualities, but the qualities are present. Furthermore, these traits are obvious to others, and they are obviously linked to the family experience.

Finally, let your children know that if your family faces the disease of alcoholism, and the problems it has caused, they can live in joy, hope, and love, even if the drinking continues.

Summary

Alcoholism is a complex and variable disease that is often misapprehended by family members and mistreated by helping professionals. Because the disease is misunderstood, it inspires great fear in those who are touched by it. This fear leads to determined efforts by the alcoholic and those close to him to deny the existence and the impact of the compulsive drinking. However, the impact is so powerful and so extensive that the family who denies it eventually becomes dishonest in nearly all phases of its existence. If you seek to reverse this pattern of systematic emotional dishonesty, you must begin by telling the truth about the alcoholism in your family and the hurt it has caused.

When your child becomes convinced that you are dealing with him honestly, and that you value and respect his feelings, he will begin to regard his own emotional experience with interest and respect. He will also become curious about, and respectful of, other people's feelings as well. He will feel free to examine and openly discuss his emotional life, and will therefore come to understand himself better. His efforts at self-understanding will help him to develop the psychological skills that are necessary for understanding others. This kind of emotional awareness is essential for your child's sense of himself as a whole person and for his development of emotional intimacy with other people.

ESTABLISHING EMOTIONAL HONESTY

- Face the alcoholic with the facts about his drinking and the facts about alcoholism
- Educate children about the *Disease Model of Alcoholism*
- Open the door to honesty with your children by expressing your own feelings about the drinking and about your role in the in the family
- Issue an explicit invitation to children to share *their* feelings, positive and negative
- Listen closely, accepting the bad as well as the good
- Conduct regular family meetings

NOTES

1 V. E. Johnson, *Intervention: How to Help Someone Who Doesn't Want Help.* (Minneapolis: Johnson Institute, 1986.)

= 6 =

Maintaining Your Emotional Stability

Therapeutic parents create an emotionally stable environment for their children by providing them with adequate emotional care in a reliable, predictable fashion. Chapter 2 explained that there are intensely *destabilizing* forces at work in an alcoholic home that hamper the efforts of recovering parents to provide reliable care for their children. This chapter highlights unstable parental behaviors and attitudes that frighten children and isolate them emotionally. It also describes behaviors that instill a feeling of confidence in children and help them to feel that they can count on their parents for love, support, and protection.

Of course, no parent is perfectly reliable, or completely predictable. As always, we strive to be "good enough" at meeting our children's needs. In this case, the goal is to provide enough emotional care and guidance, with as much consistency as possible, so that your children will feel that it is safe to be children, and safe to have and express the extraordinary emotional needs that are necessarily part of their childishness.

The Recovering Alcoholic Parent

If you are in the early stages of recovery, your sobriety must be your first priority. It is the key to regaining or acquiring the self-understanding and self-control that you will need to build a secure and stable environment for your children. Every recovery is somewhat different. Since subtle biochemical changes may continue to occur for several months after you stop drinking, you may not feel physically better for a year or more. It may also be some time before you feel significantly better emotionally. In fact, you may feel worse without alcohol, as the painful feelings you have been blocking with this powerful euphoriant return with a vengeance. This rebounding of chemically suppressed emotion is frequently a cause of relapse. It is also a source of stress and conflict in the family. You and your spouse should read the section in this chapter concerning *Fatigue, Self-Recrimination, and Aggression* together, and discuss ways to manage the tension that will undoubtedly continue after you stop drinking.

As you do begin to feel better, however, your focus will naturally shift away from the day-to-day struggle to stay sober and sane. Your energy will increase and you will begin to concentrate, to a greater degree, on the condition of your family, and the emotional struggles that your spouse and children are experiencing. At this point, you may feel a great temptation to rush to their assistance, to make promises about the future that will cheer them on, and to provide material comforts and family experiences that you hope will assuage their grief and anger. Your family, sensing that you are now more emotionally aware and available, may also press you to make up for lost time.

You once felt a compelling need to deny the extent and the destructiveness of your drinking. There is now a danger that your heightened sensitivity to your family's pain will trigger intense feelings of guilt and shame and lead you to deny the difficulty of getting better. For a very extended period, you will need to devote the bulk of your time and your attention to recovery. That is, you will need to concentrate on maintaining your sobriety, and developing a more complete understanding of yourself, your drinking, and your approach to intimate relationships.

Your recovery cannot be hurried without endangering your sobriety and, therefore, your family's stability. Veterans of Alcoholics Anonymous, who recognize that intimate relationships are as distracting and stressful as they are rewarding, typically counsel new members of the program to refrain from establishing new romantic ties for at least a year after they enter the program. You won't withdraw from your spouse and children during the first year of recovery, but you must try to remind yourself and you must allow others to remind you that your chief priority is still sobriety. It is tempting, but dangerous, to promise more than you can deliver in terms of time, attention, care, and reasonableness. Your years of drinking and the intensity of your struggle to stop drinking have strained your physical and emotional resources and reduced your ability to tolerate stress smoothly. It will probably feel embarrassing, and you will probably feel selfish when you say to yourself and your family that even though you have several months of sobriety behind you, you must continue to place recovery activities at the top of your list of priorities. However, it is better to take this position than to overextend yourself and place your family back on the old alcoholic roller coaster of elevated hopes and crushing disappointments. This would intensify their pain, and it would lead to renewed feelings of failure, shame, and guilt for you. These are precisely the sorts of feelings that increase your risk of relapse. If you are thinking about making a significant change in your recovery program to accommodate your family, or to suit any other purpose, it is a good idea to spend some time reflecting on your progress and your present treatment needs with your AA sponsor and/or a professional addictions counselor.

If your children want more than you feel able to give during the early part of your recovery, and you feel ashamed of your limitations, you may find yourself trying to shift the responsibility for this conflict onto them. You may withdraw from your children, or criticize them for making demands, all the while implying that there is something fundamentally wrong about their desire for your care and companionship. When a parent tells a child that his need for love is immature and selfish, the child almost always believes this, even though this need is perfectly normal and healthy. If the child is pushed away and punished too often for the things he craves from his parents, he will become ashamed of his need to depend on others, and will try to be a "big kid" who takes care of his problems and needs all by himself. He may grow up feeling that he doesn't deserve love and cut himself off from the possibility of real intimacy and care from others.

On the other hand, you will greatly strengthen your child's sense of himself and his self-worth if you can explain to him that it is your own limitations that are infringing on your relationship with him. Try to describe the demands of recovery in simple terms and then acknowledge that his need for you is natural, as is his disappointment when you are unavailable. You want to convey to him that with all his longing, frustration, and anger, he makes sense to you, and is perfectly all right with you. The reason for any distance, or tension in your relationship with him is not that he is alienating you with his hunger for your presence, but that you are struggling to regain your health, so that you can be a full-time parent once again.

In general, it is always a good idea to keep children informed about what you're doing in your recovery program. When they have facts about your illness and your treatment, they will be relieved of the necessity to invent explanations for your emotional ups and downs and odd comings and goings. However alarming the facts of the situation are, they are almost never as disturbing as the fantastic theories of children in troubled homes, who usually see themselves as the perpetrator of high crimes that are about to shatter the family.

Furthermore, your attempt to recover your health and sobriety is a courageous act. Pain and adversity come to everyone during life, and the memory of a parent who stood up to great challenge and conquered it is an invaluable source of inspiration to children as they struggle to master their own conflicts. The more they know about your commitment to, and active pursuit of change, the more they will be able to use you as a heroic model.

If your children have weathered several seasons of hope and disappointment about your drinking, they will bring a heavy burden of resentment and hurt to this present recovery effort, and it will probably be some time before they believe in the durability of your sobriety. However, as they notice that you are becoming more responsive to their feelings, that you are struggling to control your anger, and that you are more emotionally vulnerable than you have been in recent memory, your children are likely to become much more vocal about their pain, including their anger. They may not voice their distress about your drinking directly, but even if they seem to challenge you over trivial matters, the source of their rage is very likely to be your alcoholism and the ways in which it has hurt the family. Since your own feelings, especially your feelings of guilt and shame, are closer to the surface now, you may find that you are easily and deeply wounded by their criticism. In the past you probably anesthetized this kind of hurt with alcohol, or repelled it with a rageful counterattack. Your goal as a therapeutic parent, however, is to remain stable and predictable with your children even when they assault your self-esteem. You must not turn the tables by attacking them, but, rather, you should work with them toward a resolution of the pain that exists between you.

How to Have a Fair Fight

Working with and helping a child to manage his anger means listening closely to his complaints. However, you do not have to be, nor should you be, a passive recipient of a rageful outburst. This stormy period with your child presents an opportunity for the entire family to master the rules of fair fighting and active listening. The topic of active listening is covered in the next chapter, which discusses ways to create an atmosphere of emotional responsiveness in your home. The basic rules of fair fighting, which you can practice and then teach your child, are as follows:

- When making a complaint, do not accuse others, or attribute feelings to them. Rather, use "I" statements and talk about what's going on in your head, and your heart. Say, "I think, I feel, I need..."
  - Don't say: "You're trying to hurt me by staying out so late without calling."
  - Try: "I get very worried when you're out so late and I haven't heard from you and have no idea where you are."

- Do not condemn someone's character by making sweeping generalizations about his behavior. You must be very careful about this. Even when your child says something hateful, you must remain respectful of him. This is what will make him feel safe enough to examine his own feelings, and to share his real problems with you. Furthermore, it will help him to follow the rules for fighting that you are trying to establish. He won't behave like a street fighter once he's sure he's not in the street. So, instead of meeting an angry challenge with an attack on your child's self-esteem, be specific about the behavior that you object to. *Describe it precisely and describe your emotional reaction to it.*
  - Don't say: "You always let me down. Can't you get your mind off yourself for awhile?"
  - Try: "I was really depending on you to help me with dinner tonight. When you forget your promises like that, I start to think my feelings aren't important to you."
- If you feel that you are about to lose control, and become verbally or physically abusive, call a time-out. It is no more constructive to argue when you're enraged than it is to argue when you're drunk.
- Affirm your child's right to be angry with you. Remember that concerns that seem trivial to you may well be the tip of an iceberg that contains all of his feelings about your drinking. Even if you can't see any justification for his complaints, give him the benefit of the doubt. You can say, "I'm sure if you're this upset there must be something important bothering you. Let's keep talking until we both understand what it is."
- Take turns talking. No one should be allowed to interrupt anyone else.
- Don't remind your child of mistakes he committed in the past.
- Make sure you understand the point your child is trying to make. Restate the idea he has expressed and ask him if you've got it right. If he says no, ask him to try and tell you what he means again. Then restate the point once more and ask him if you've got it this time. This process may feel tedious to you, but if you stick with it until you both understand exactly what issues are under discussion, you'll save a lot of confusion and a lot of hurt feelings. We always listen with a selective ear, because we hope to hear something that is pleasing, or because we expect to hear something familiar. Your child needs you to try and get past these filters, and to make contact with what is really happening inside him.
- When the process of fair fighting does feel tedious, or too frightening to continue, try to remember that, as the last chapter explained,

an open and honest exchange of feelings is one of the most important goals for a recovering family. It is a sign that everyone is getting better when suppressed pain begins to be exposed, and family members start to examine their feelings together. Your child's sense of well-being and emotional integrity depends on his belief that he is free to be himself, and express his true reactions to events in the family. He will only believe that such freedom exists when he is sure that, no matter what he feels or says, he will continue to have your love and respect.

Finally, as long as your recovery is causing you substantial physical and emotional pain, you will long for care and support from others, and you should have it. However, you must expect that most of this assistance will come from members of your recovery program and from professional helpers. Your spouse and children may or may not be able to understand your pain. But even if they are not actively angry with you right now and express a wish to help you, their distress is as profound as yours and their recoveries as complex and demanding. It is important that you restrain your child if he attempts to "parent" you. If he seems too preoccupied with your welfare, gently remind him to keep his sights set on his own recovery. He will feel reassured if you thank him for his care and concern, yet explain that you are getting a great deal of help from your recovery activities. Older children should, of course, be encouraged to attend Alateen.

THE RULES OF FAIR FIGHTING

- Affirm your child's right to feel angry
- Never condemn your child's character
- Make *specific* complaints—describe the behavior you dislike in objective terms
- Use "I" statements to describe your reactions to your child's behavior
- Take time-outs as necessary

The Recovering Codependent Parent

> For a long time, I thought all my problems stemmed from my father's drinking. I now think my mother's reaction to his drinking created a lot of problems for me. For one thing, she absorbed all this abuse from him without a peep. And she let him push us around too. This made me feel that women, especially me, are worthless, and that they have to take anything from a man. The other thing that happened, that really ended up hurting me a lot, is that living with him made her hate herself. And a lot of that self-hate got dumped onto me.
>
> *Marie—Age forty-three*

A parent demonstrates emotional stability when he maintains his fundamental values and perspectives during periods of intense stress, even if that stress poses grave challenges to his self-esteem. Many partners of alcoholics assume that to maintain a stable emotional environment, they must also "manage" the problem drinking so that the alcoholic and the family appear to be functioning normally. Unfortunately, if you try to "manage" your spouse's alcoholism by concealing it and compensating for it, you will have only the illusion of stability and control.

Alcoholism does not respond to delaying tactics or evasive maneuvers. It will succumb only to a full-scale frontal assault. Anything short of an all-out effort to defeat this disease provides an opportunity for it to become more firmly established in the body of the alcoholic, and more deeply embedded in the soul of the family. This is why addiction professionals, and the Anonymous programs, say that a co-alcoholic's efforts to manage compulsive drinking actually "enables" it to continue.

Furthermore, children in alcoholic homes look to their sober parent for the sanity and security that they must have and that the actively alcoholic parent is incapable of providing. If you drink with the alcoholic, cover for her, minimize or justify her destructive behavior, attempt to regulate her intake of liquor, or deny that she needs help, you will lose your children's trust and respect. Children rightly conclude that an actively codependent, enabling parent constitutes a flimsy barrier against the destructiveness of the alcoholic. They begin to feel that they are all alone with their pain and fear. Many children take from this experience a feeling of vulnerability and endangerment that will remain with them all their lives.

Your Sobriety Is Essential

It is especially important that you remain sober. Many partners of active alcoholics, especially those who cannot, or will not, turn to outside sources of comfort and assistance, come to feel overwhelmed by their daily conflicts with the drinker and by their incessant interior struggle with feelings of grief, anger, fear, and loneliness. Many turn to compulsive pursuits of their own in an effort to relieve their pain. You may find that you are making excuses to drink with your alcoholic. A shared drinking episode not only results in temporary respite from your battles with the drinker, and with yourself, but also affords an opportunity to "keep an eye" on your spouse and perhaps to feel some sense of connection with her.

On the other hand, you may despise the thought of participating in behavior that has brought you such terrible torment, but gratefully accept anti-anxiety or sleeping medications prescribed by physicians who have misunderstood, or else simply mistreated, the signs of chronic stress that co-alcoholics commonly exhibit. A harmful dependency is likely to develop in either case since the emotional pressure on you is unrelenting, and since both drugs afford a dramatic, if relatively fleeting, release from this state of emotional siege.

Alcoholism and prescription drug abuse are the addictive illnesses that most often afflict codependent spouses, but you must understand that you are vulnerable to compulsive problems of all kinds, including eating disorders, workaholism, and uncontrolled spending. Since denial is a universal symptom of compulsive illness, it will be difficult to examine yourself for signs of an incipient addiction. On the other hand, most addicts, in the early stages of their disease, question their compulsive behavior and its meaning. Most, in fact, are so troubled by it, that they make repeated, if short-lived, efforts to eliminate it. When these early efforts at recovery fail, it is usually because the need for the compulsive object is very strong, and the addict tries to manage her need alone.

If you find yourself questioning the way in which you use alcohol or other drugs, or if you worry that your approach to work or food is unhealthy, your challenge, as usual, is to reach outside yourself for help. In this case, you need someone to help you gain perspective as to the gravity of your problem, and to provide support and direction as you attempt to address it. It is vital that you, as the spouse of an alcoholic, fight for your own recovery with whatever means you can muster.

Compulsions are, by their very nature, anti-intimate. An emotionally intimate exchange involves honest disclosure of some critically important aspect of yourself to another person. Any substantial, heartfelt emotion presses upward and outward for this kind of release. If you are too frightened to expose authentic feelings in an intimate exchange with another human being, you will probably turn to some compulsive activity in an effort to escape this intense internal pressure.

Yet your children must have intimate emotional contact with you if they are to feel loved and worthy of love. Only by revealing the truest part of themselves, and sensing its importance and meaning for you, will they come to believe in their own value. If your experiences with your spouse, and perhaps with your own parents and siblings, have made you fearful of emotional intimacy, and you are withdrawing into a compulsion, your children will not be able to develop this kind of connection with you. Your perception of their feelings, as well as your own, will be distorted and you will be unable to share your emotional life with them or respond appropriately to their emotional needs.

Protecting Your Children from Emotional Abuse

Another form of enabling could badly undermine your child's sense of your emotional stability, and your capacity to provide reliable care. A child's sense of security is profoundly shaken when a sober parent, who is frightened that a confrontation with the alcoholic may trigger a violent outburst or a binge, fails to intervene when the alcoholic is hurting the child. The problem of child abuse and child endangerment is covered in chapter 8, which presents strategies for ensuring your child's physical security. But it is also important that you, as the sober parent, intervene on behalf of your child if she is being subjected to emotional harassment and verbal abuse.

Most alcoholics cope with feelings of self-hatred by displacing them onto family members. Children are frequently targeted for this kind of attack, since they usually lack the intellectual, emotional, and physical resources to resist parental aggression. Character assassination, when it comes from a parent, is devastating to a child, who views his parents as omniscient, even when they behave irrationally and with terrible cruelty. Although the child may argue his case with vehemence and outrage when he is reviled by an abusive parent, a child almost always interprets parental abuse as a reasonable and just punishment for his bad behavior and character.

Chapter 3 discussed how a child's images of his parent and the way that his parent habitually treats him are absorbed and eventually become an active and potent part of the child's personality. The child whose self-image is founded on a mental picture of his persecution by an abusive parent may struggle throughout life with feelings of worthlessness and helplessness. This is one way that self-esteem is progressively and severely damaged in alcoholic homes. However, if you quickly and firmly move to your child's defense when he is being tormented by your alcoholic spouse, you will help him to avoid this painful outcome. The love and respect you convey through your protective maneuver will shield him from the present harm, and it will also furnish him with the psychic resources he will need to protect himself for a lifetime. This is because an image of you as his loving defender will also become a part of him. Whenever his self-esteem is threatened in the future, he will be able to summon the memory of your loving and protective voice to help him repel bad feelings about himself—whether they arise from within him or are activated by destructive people he encounters in his dealings with the outside world. Your child will successfully defend himself because you cared enough to defend him in his struggle with his abusive parent.

Fatigue, Self-Recrimination, and Aggression

Chronic fatigue, deep-seated feelings of frustration, disappointment, anger, hurt, and fear, are the most usual legacy of an extended battle with the bottle. This is true for the drinker, even if she has initiated recovery activities, and it is true for the codependent, sober spouse as well. Another painful emotion that commonly haunts adults in alcoholic families is self-contempt. Compulsive drinkers despise themselves because they recognize, if only at an unconscious level, the damage they have done to their bodies, their minds, and their families. The codependent spouse accuses himself because he is unable to keep the alcoholic from drinking. Sometimes he believes that he has caused the drinking. Both partners feel worse as the disease grows more severe. What's more, the inhibitions and perspective of both deteriorate as they become more physically, and emotionally, fatigued. Soldiers who serve too long in a combat zone finally break down, and the alcoholic and co-alcoholic eventually become incapable of containing their anguish as well.

If you have been pressed beyond your psychological limits, you may begin to displace your most disturbing feelings, including self-contempt, onto your children. In time, it may become reflexive and habitual to view your children as the source of your family's problems.

If you are a codependent parent, you may feel that your children's bad behavior, or their constant need for care, are causing the alcoholic's reckless and hurtful behavior. One woman felt degraded by her alcoholic husband's extramarital escapades, but could not confront his behavior directly. Some of her husband's paramours were members of the couple's immediate circle of friends, and although the wife was well aware of their identities, she would sometimes entertain them in her home. She was the very soul of discretion and dignity on such occasions, but later, when she was alone with her daughter, she would assault the child with accusations of physical and characterological ugliness. Her mother's condemnation was harder for the daughter to dismiss than her father's frequent absences, and his embarrassing behavior with other women. Her mother was, after all, sober. The daughter became chronically depressed. As an adult she was habitually involved with men who berated and shamed her.

Countless numbers of children from alcoholic homes grow to adulthood with the memory of being denounced by their sober parent. They feel helpless to reconcile, or to set aside the judgment of their "healthy" parent, who declared them fatally deficient.

MIKE

Mike was thirteen when his father, who had been drinking alcoholically for years, suddenly stopped. He doesn't know what inspired his dad to "take the pledge," as his mother put it, but he does remember that the family's sense of relief and pleasure about his father's transformation was tainted by their dread that something would happen to upset the precarious applecart of his newfound sobriety.

When Mike turned fourteen in the Spring, his father was still sober, and his mother asked Mike if he had any ideas about how the family might celebrate his birthday. Mike missed the big family outings that had been a regular feature of family life before his father's drinking had grown so severe in the last two years, and he asked if the family might go out to dinner together in honor of his birthday. As soon as he made this request, he sensed his mother's distress. And he knew why his plan was so unsettling to her. She was, of course, afraid that when Mike's father found himself in a fancy restaurant with something to celebrate, he would order a drink. Mike's father seized on the idea of the celebration dinner and insisted on fulfilling Mike's birthday wish. He did order the drink, and, in fact, fell into a full-scale relapse.

Obviously, Mike's father was on shaky ground at the time Mike made his birthday request, and it was only a matter of time until he found an excuse to resume drinking. But Mike's mother told him, time and again, that he was to blame for his father's relapse. Since his father ultimately died of his alcoholism, this accusation has been a deeply troubling one for Mike. And his mother held him responsible for other deficits and disappointments that she felt as well. Though he is now grown, and lives several hundred miles away from his mother, he struggles daily with oppressive feelings of guilt and shame.

It is easy, when reading stories such as Mike's, to see the injustice of the adult's behavior, and to imagine the grave injury to a child whose parents charge him with the destruction of the family. It is substantially harder to check an actual outburst of psychological, or physical aggression when you are living with the intense and chronic pain of active alcoholism, and you are struggling with your own burden of guilt and shame. Codependent and recovering adults under this kind of pressure often rail at a child with very little awareness of the harm that is being inflicted. If you can acknowledge, however, that you are living in a condition of chronic psychic trauma, and that you *must* have some constructive way in which to discharge your pain, you can avoid establishing or perpetuating this destructive pattern with your children.

If you are living with an active alcoholic or a recovering alcoholic with a shaky sobriety, much of your inner distress is a reaction to your spouse's drinking, or to your apprehension that she will drink. Unless you fear for your physical safety, some of this distress should be expressed to her. As any veteran of Al-Anon knows, this does not mean that you should badger, revile, or plead with your spouse about her drinking. It does mean that you should level with her, when she is sober, about your desire for change in the family, about your intention to get help, and about your expectation that she will get help as well.

But there must be other outlets for your pain. These might include Al-Anon and personal counseling, as well as exchanges with understanding and accepting friends. When you speak with a counselor or friend, or when you share at a Twelve-Step meeting, it is important to express, as directly and honestly as you can, your feelings of vulnerability, self-doubt, and fear. If you try to keep a stiff upper lip, and to pretend that you have your home situation well in hand, you will heighten the internal tension that can lead to a psychological or even a physical assault on a child.

If you are in the first, arduous year of recovery from your own drinking problem, you, like your spouse, will be struggling with feelings of guilt, shame, fear, and insecurity. What's more, you will be doing so at a time when you are physically debilitated. Your need for support during this period is also very great.

Unfortunately, the denial that is part and parcel of the family disease of alcoholism alienates alcoholics and codependents alike from their most heartfelt emotions, especially feelings of need and fear. If you grew up in an alcoholic home yourself, you are even more likely to try to deny your longings for support, love, and understanding. You may put your shoulder to the wheel and press on, even as your despair and terror rise. However, your need for comfort actually intensifies as you push it aside. It will inevitably push back and press for expression. If you, like so many adults from alcoholic homes, have learned to despise your need for help from others, you are likely to become extremely afraid and extremely self-condemning as these feelings grow in you. It is this condition of intense fear and irrational self-censure that places you at risk for an act of aggression against your children. This is why it is so crucial to relieve internal tension by expressing need to others. It is also extremely helpful to ask others to reassure you that your desire for help is normal, and indeed, universal.

It Is Therapeutic to Acknowledge Error

Parents naturally feel guilty and ashamed when they realize that they have brought their children undeserved pain. Of course, it is the rare parent who has not done this, and who has not made other mistakes as well. It is important for parents to understand that when they commit these errors, they are acting out of inner torment and not inner evil. But it is also critical that parents make every effort to avoid inflicting further abuse. Parents Anonymous is a Twelve-Step Program that is enormously helpful to parents who are striving to reverse a cycle of verbal or physical aggression against their children. The toll-free phone number for this organization is 1-800-421-0353.

Finally, it is never too late for a parent to apologize for past mistakes. It will be strengthening to your child and to the relationship between you if you make him aware of the fact that you have recognized an error in your treatment of him, that you regret it, and that you have made a commitment to change. Your own parents may have shamed you for your mistakes, and made you feel that flaws in your personality or behavior are tantamount to your failure as a human being. If so, or if you fear that it will undermine your authority with your children, or even frighten them if you admit a serious mistake, it will be very hard for you to apologize.

However, mistakes are not the same as failure and they are inherent in our humanity. We do not protect our children when we conceal and deny our imperfections. Rather, we perpetuate an ethic of impossibly high expectations and condemn our children to repeat our own struggles with shame and self-recrimination. On the other hand, if we admit our mistakes, remain relatively calm about the fact that we have committed them, and display a sense of determination about changing our behavior, it helps our children to develop an attitude of self-acceptance about their own faults, and also instills in them a feeling of confidence about the possibility of overcoming these.

It is also profoundly comforting and affirming to a child when a parent acknowledges a wrongful act and expresses sincere regret about having caused him real pain. In most cases, children blame themselves for anything that goes badly with a parent, and it is immensely relieving to them to have this burden of shame and guilt lifted from their shoulders.

Summary

Therapeutic parents work for emotional stability. That is, they strive to maintain their sensibility, sensitivity, and self-control, even when they feel bad. Perfect stability is quite impossible for parents to achieve, even in the best of circumstances. And in alcoholic homes, even during active recovery efforts, there is intense pressure on parents' feelings of well-being and self-esteem. Even very good parents will sometimes behave erratically and destructively under this pressure. But, with adequate social and emotional support, recovering parents can provide enough stability to renew a child's feeling of trust and emotional ease.

THE STABLE PARENT

- Remains sober
- Protects his child—not family secrets
- Shares his feelings of struggle with other adults, so that pain and fatigue will not be transformed into unpredictable rage
- Acknowledges and apologizes for inevitable lapses

≡ 7 ≡

Being Emotionally Responsive to Your Children

NICHOLAS

I grew up in a "stiff-upper-lip" type of family. If you were hurting, you kept it to yourself, or Mom and Dad and the other kids let you know you were being a real baby. My wife has been drinking heavily for about five years now. Everybody in our family hurts real bad. The kids especially. They argue all the time and cry for their Mommy when she doesn't come home. I don't know what to do. I'd feel like a bum if I told the girls what my parents said to me: Be strong. Don't complain. Big kids don't cry. But what should I tell them when they're upset? I feel like I don't have a clue.

The chief priority of a recovering parent must be abstinence. Your emotional and physical health and that of your children depends absolutely on your commitment not to drink and not to enable drinking. However, full recovery from familial alcoholism involves much more than abstinence from alcohol and from the compulsive and destructive behaviors that grow up around chemical addiction. Stable abstinence provides a foundation for psychic and spiritual renewal, but it cannot fulfill these ends.

A deep, full feeling of humanity and the experience of joy and meaning in life require a firm sense of personal value, as well as a belief in one's future prospects for love, care, and respect from others.

Unfortunately, self-esteem and hope for the future take a severe beating in actively alcoholic homes. Everyone feels ashamed of how the family is living, and each family member feels somehow responsible for the problem. At the same time, no one feels powerful enough or smart enough to combat the malignant forces that are at work in the family. As a recovering parent, you may have successfully stemmed the growth and spread of your own despair, but you are probably struggling, every day, to hold the ground you've gained. Still, you face another daunting challenge: How are you to provide encouragement and inspiration to your children?

Emotional Patterns in Alcoholic Homes

Children feel important, lovable, and hopeful in proportion to their ability to inspire love in their parents. Children, especially younger ones who have become painfully aware of their vulnerability in the world, take frequent and regular stock of their position in the family. They evaluate their status according to the quantity and kind of emotional attention they receive from their parents. And whereas children are certainly interested in what parents have to say about the love they feel, they are more vitally concerned with how their parents behave toward them. Parents who are drinking alcoholically, or who are attempting to manage the drinking of a spouse, often behave in ways that make children feel emotionally disregarded or emotionally abused.

Some children in alcoholic families find that it is hard to kindle any kind of emotional response in their parents. In many cases, parents are almost completely absorbed and exhausted by their conflicts with alcohol and each other. And sometimes, even nondrinking codependent parents turn to cigarettes, tranquilizers, or some other emotionally deadening object in an effort to ease their emotional pain. As they retreat further into the fog of some personal anesthesia, they become numb to their children's feelings and needs.

Children feel lonely and frightened when their overburdened parents retreat inside themselves. They feel guilty, ashamed, and worthless when their parents discharge overwhelming feelings of conflict, shame, and self-contempt by staging a rageful assault on them (see the section in chapter 6 entitled: *Fatigue, Self-Recrimination, and Aggression*). When parents turn to them for emotional support and care, children feel pressured, insecure, and emotionally overwhelmed.

When one or more of these dysfunctional emotional patterns arises in an alcoholic family, it often persists even after abstinence has been established. This is especially true if parents do not have a formal program of recovery to help them identify hurtful behaviors that are associated with alcoholism and codependency. Force of habit is one factor that fuels destructive emotional cycles in recovering families. However, recovering parents also continue to feel bad once they have given up compulsive drinking and enabling behaviors. Abstinence creates its own problems, including an increased sensitivity to emotional pain. Human beings tend to fall back on primitive coping mechanisms when they are faced with severe physical or emotional stress. You may find that you want to strike out or run away when you're feeling especially bad. However neither of these strategies is very helpful to a child who is also in pain. All children, especially those who are fighting for a sense of value and purpose, need parents who can provide positive and consistent emotional attention, even during troubled times.

The Art of Empathy

Training programs require aspiring mental health professionals to spend an enormous amount of learning to empathize with their clients. This is because experienced helpers understand that clients are largely uninterested in the help of any counselor who does not truly understand their feelings. The feeling of being understood—deeply and thoroughly understood—is the most humanizing and hopeful of interpersonal experiences, and the effort to understand is perhaps the most persuasive evidence of real love.

Empathy is a process that sounds simple, but it can be very difficult to achieve, especially when you, as a listener, are under emotional pressure. Empathy is not the same as sympathy, although the effort to empathize with another always implies compassion for that person's emotional experience. And empathy amounts to a great deal more than simple intellectual understanding of the other person's feelings. When you fully empathize with another human being, you actually experience a part of what he is feeling. You may feel teary or hurt as he describes grief over a painful loss; or find yourself getting hot under the collar when he recounts a tale of unfair punishment.

Empathy is not a *reaction to* another person, it is a matter of *reacting with* another person to some important event. Most of us have felt this kind of deep connection with someone before. You may experience it frequently or it may be a relatively rare occurrence in your life. Perhaps you have found that feelings of affinity and shared understanding occur without any conscious effort on your part. Very often, these feelings are triggered by a dramatic encounter with someone who has had an experience that is similar to some important event in our own lives. As we listen to the other person's story, we spontaneously release the feelings in ourselves that are associated with our original experience.

Spontaneous empathic connections can be exciting, and even transforming. However, parents, especially parents in recovering families, cannot afford to wait and hope that such connections will develop. Parents must learn to concentrate their attention on a child's emotional world so that they are able, with some cooperation from the child, to participate in his day-to-day emotional life. It is this ongoing interest and responsiveness from a parent that leads a child to feel more important, more supported, and more loved.

You can take several steps to improve your empathy skills, your ability to "tune in" to your child. Practicing these steps will help you and your child to feel more solidly and more deeply connected. You'll be more in touch with his daily ups and downs, and you will also be able to respond more quickly and effectively when your child is in an emotional crisis.

Making Feelings Important in Your Home

As a therapeutic parent seeking to strengthen your emotional bond with your child, you must assign feelings and emotional needs a high priority in your home and actively encourage their expression. You can't "tune in" to your child unless he is sending out at least some strong, and fairly direct emotional signals. Children in alcoholic families often conceal and disguise their feelings because they're afraid they'll get punished or badly disappointed if they reveal too much to a troubled parent. Chapter 5 explained how family meetings can be used to get people in recovering families to talk to one another more directly and honestly. In this forum, and whenever people are talking about how they feel, emotions and emotional needs should be accorded great respect. They are just as important as achievements that make everyone feel proud, and they deserve as much consideration as pressing financial problems or physical pains and ailments that family members are suffering. Each family member should be invited and encouraged to express his or her needs in an appropriate way, and when any member asks for assistance or support he or she should be praised for having the good sense and courage to reach out for help. No one should be ridiculed or criticized for expressing vulnerability or requesting aid.

Working Through Emotional Pain and Conflict

In a home in which feelings are expressed freely and often, there will inevitably be conflict. And in a recovering family, in which members are becoming more honest about how they feel, grief and anger about the past will certainly be expressed. The venting of emotional pain and conflict is normal, and it is necessary for emotional growth. As individuals, we perceive the world in different ways and have different ways of getting our most important needs met. Furthermore, we all experience anxiety, depression, and anger from time to time. It is unrealistic to attempt to eliminate conflict and emotional pain from our lives. Rather, we must find ways to resolve our pain and to manage conflict in a fair and rational way if we desire lasting and meaningful relationships with other people.

Conflict that is fueled by, and conducted in an atmosphere of intoxication and alcoholic thinking is usually not resolved in a fair and rational way. On the contrary, it usually leads to emotional or physical abuse. Therefore, when members of a recovering family express negative, conflictual feelings, they may well feel frightened that their emotional exchanges will end, not with a feeling of satisfaction and resolution but rather with greater pain. You can allay your children's fears of expressing controversial feelings and needs by explaining that conflict in close relationships is normal, healthy, and productive, and by expressing your own conflicts with other family members in an appropriate and open way. When conflicts arise, try always to follow the rules of fair fighting described in chapter 6. The fundamental principles of fair fighting, are, once again:

- There will be no physical or verbal abuse when family members confront one another, or when they disagree.
- There will be an honest and concerted effort to meet some needs of each person involved in the conflict.
- At the very least, each person's need to be heard, acknowledged, and respected will be honored.

Modeling Self-Respect and Self-Care

Your children will become more interested in their feelings, more compassionate toward them, and more candid about them if you consistently demonstrate a respectful concern for your own emotional world. Even if your children frequently refuse to do what you tell them to do, they will almost certainly grow up emulating a great many of your characteristic behaviors and attitudes. If you are able to renounce compulsive activities that stifle and distort your feelings, and if you can begin to actively pursue emotional freedom and intimacy, this will have an enormous impact on the way your children conduct their own lives. The following are some general principles of self-respect and self-care that therapeutic parents should observe to instill in children a healthy regard for feelings and emotional needs.

- Resist exploitation and abuse from any source, including your employers, your partner, your friends, your parents, and your children.

- When you are struggling with indecision, confusion, and self-destructive behaviors, address your pain in a timely and direct way: Get support from peers and secure professional help when it is indicated.
- Make the pursuit of emotional intimacy, within and outside the family, a high priority:
  - Be consistent and careful in your attempts to understand your partner and your children, and ask that they do the same. (See *Becoming an Active Listener.*)
  - Develop and maintain a friendship and support network outside the family.
  - Encourage your children to form alliances and friendships outside the family.

Becoming an Active Listener

NICHOLAS

Life in our family has become a grim proposition I guess. Since my wife, Anne, and I both work, there's always a lot to do, and not nearly enough time to do it in. Now she's at meetings seven nights a week, so that's a pair of hands missing.

Last Saturday, while my wife was at a noon time meeting, the girls got into an awful row about chores—you know, "It's your turn to clean the bathroom!," and, "Oh no it's not! It's your turn!" That's all I hear from them any more, and I'm feeling like I just can't take this stuff right now. I mean, this is really what I need, right? I'm at the end of my rope as it is, going from crisis to crisis with Anne, and all these two brats can do is argue. So I really blew up. Told them both what a shame it is they can't help out a little when I work all week, and I sent them to their rooms. I was really fuming for awhile, but then, I got to thinking, they're not really brats. They don't usually fuss like that, just like I don't usually lose my temper that fast. We're just all stretched so thin. So I went upstairs to see them, and just commented about how we were all acting pretty wound up and I wondered what was going on. Sharon started to cry and said that it seems we never have any fun any more. It's just work and school and come home and do more work. Katherine said the same kind of thing. Actually, she said she wonders if we'll ever laugh again. I said I understood that. That it does seem like a long time since we've had any laughs. That it seems we've been worrying and thinking about Mommy for a real long time. Then Sharon said, "She's never here! First she was out drinking all the time. And now that she's supposed to be getting well, she's still never home!" Katherine chimes in and says, "Why doesn't she help us a little? Why do we have to do everything ourselves?" And then I saw it very clearly. They miss her. Just like I do. They're lonely and scared and angry all the time, just like I am. And that's why we're all fighting and sulking all the time.

The ability to empathize with others depends on the quality of our listening skills. Most of us think we know how to listen, but communication, especially communication that contains strong, perhaps disturbing, emotional information, is a very complicated process. For one thing, people send out nonverbal messages that can be every bit as important as verbal ones, and the things they do may even contradict the things they say.

Consider the following universal, maddening experience. You come upon your child in a state of obvious sadness and dejection. He's sitting on his bed, staring at the floor and surreptitiously wiping tears from his eyes. Alarmed, you ask, "What's wrong?" He responds, of course, by saying, "Nothing."

If you attend only to your child's verbal message, you will obviously miss a great deal of important emotional information. If you consider the fact that his face is a mask of pain and that he cannot meet your eyes, and press the issue by saying, "I can see that something's wrong. What is it?" you will very likely trigger an angry outburst. "I said nothing's wrong! Leave me alone!"

You've seen the hurt on your child's face and you've heard his angry words. You've listened, in the sense of hearing all that was said and watching all that was done. Chances are, however, you're still not sure what you're dealing with here. Is this an angry child? A sad one? Could he be frightened, like you used to be, of telling his parents what's bothering him? Is he feeling all these things, and something more?

Children send out complicated and confusing emotional messages all the time. They're not deliberately attempting to confound us. They are genuinely mixed up about what's going on inside their heads and their hearts. Even young children have very complex reactions to situations they encounter in the family and in the larger world outside the family. However, they are not very experienced and not at all adept at sorting out and describing their feelings. Whereas older children may be more emotionally sophisticated, they will still have trouble analyzing their reactions to a great life crisis. And there is no greater crisis for a child than a parent who is out of control.

The goal of a therapeutic parent who is trying to understand a confused child is to help that child sort out his own confusion. Once this is accomplished, parent *and* child will have a clearer picture of what the child is feeling. Furthermore, the child will not feel alone with his problems. Active listening is a powerful tool you can employ as you try to assist your child in gaining a keener awareness of himself.

Don't Ask Questions. The first principle of active listening is to abandon, as much as possible, the technique of posing questions to your child. Children generally feel pressured when they're being questioned by an adult, because adults are bigger and more powerful, because they often ask questions in an anxious tone (that the child hears as disapproving), and because they seem to assume that the child has, or should have, an answer to the question being posed. A child who feels on the defensive with a parent thinks defensively, to the extent that he can think clearly at all. He thinks about how he can conceal whatever it is he knows, instead of considering how he might express what is inside.

Reserve Judgment. The second important principle of active listening is to suspend critical judgment during conversations that are intended to increase emotional contact between you and your child. Children are acutely sensitive to parental disapproval and anxiety, and they shut down quickly as soon as they feel either coming their way. If you are talking with your child and he says something that upsets or frightens you, you will naturally want to address it once you really know how he feels about it and you've had time to think through your own feelings about it. You'll have the time and space to explore your child's attitudes and yours more fully if you can hold on to your feelings and opinions, even as you feel your temper or your anxiety rise. It is even important to withhold reassurance when you sense that your child may have more to say about a disturbing subject. Reassurance tends to close off a discussion. It is better to use your active listening techniques and keep the conversation going until you have the whole story.

Use Active Listening Techniques. The active listening techniques include:
- Restatement
- Reflection
- Summarization

Verbal tracking maneuvers are the first skills taught to budding mental health professionals in graduate school, and they are often prescribed to couples who enter marital therapy because of a breakdown in communication. They provide a gentle, non-intrusive means of following another person's train of thought. Most children are more inclined to share their thoughts and feelings when their parents use restatement, reflection, and summarization because these techniques serve to invite, rather than command, self-examination and expression. They convey interest, as opposed to anxiety and suspicion. As your child shares more of his inner experience, you will understand him better and be better able to express your understanding to him. This will strengthen the positive bond between you.

Restatement. Restatement is the easiest active listening technique to master, and yet it is still quite powerful. To use restatement, you simply reiterate, as precisely as you can, an important phrase, sentence, or idea that your child has expressed. This allows you to check whether you have, in fact, correctly heard what he is trying to say, and it also demonstrates that you are trying hard to listen and understand.

Let's consider how restatement might be used if your child asks whether you, or your spouse will ever drink again. In this situation, you may find that you are tempted to quickly reassure your youngster, even though you know that sobriety is strictly a one-day-at-a-time affair. However, an empty promise now will only serve to undermine the efforts you've made to forge a bond of trust with your child. Furthermore, you'll prematurely terminate the discussion if you rush to tell him he needn't worry. Perhaps your sobriety isn't all that's on his mind right now. Using restatement will allow you to find out how long, how much, and in what way this subject has been bothering him. It will also buy you some time to consider how you really want to answer this difficult question.

This is how such a conversation might go with the use of simple restatement and without questions or comments from the parent who is being confronted.

CHILD: Dad, do you think you'll ever drink again?
DAD: You're wondering if I'm going to drink?
CHILD: Yeah, Billy says you're a drunk, and a drunk never stops being a drunk.
DAD: Billy says I'll never get better.
CHILD: He's always ragging me about it.
DAD: He's really on your back about my drinking.
CHILD: He saw you the day you had that fight with Mr. Nathan.

DAD: He saw me really loaded.
CHILD: I think everybody was outside that day.

It quickly becomes clear that this child is concerned about his father relapsing because a "buddy" has been taunting him about a drunken brawl between the father and a neighbor. Since the father did not cut the conversation short by assuring the boy that he is confident of his sobriety, he has gained a fairly distinct picture of his son's concerns. It is possible to begin making some educated guesses about the child's emotional state. The father can check the accuracy of his presumptions by reflecting these feelings back to the boy.

Reflection of Feeling. Reflecting feelings, like restating ideas or thoughts, requires you to temporarily set aside your own reactions and judgments. Once again, you must focus your attention on your child's words and behavior. In this case, however, you should try to use the things your child says and does to help him identify and express his feelings. When you've heard enough to think you have a sense of what he's going through, check your perception of the emotional situation by reflecting or suggesting to your child what might be happening inside him.

Adding reflection of feeling to the hypothetical conversation between a recovering father and son further sharpens our view of the child's turmoil.

DAD: He saw me really loaded.
CHILD: I think everybody was outside that day.
DAD: You must have felt so embarrassed.
CHILD: Yeah. (Seems to be holding back tears.)
DAD: Those were awful times. Its OK to cry.
CHILD: (Starts to sob.) They really were, Dad. (Continues to cry, but clenches his fists and pounds his knee.) I hated it when you were drinking.
DAD: I know. I don't blame you. I'm sure you were pretty angry at me lots of times, too.
CHILD: No, Dad! You had a lot of problems back then, work and worrying about me and Mom and everything. I know that.
DAD: My problem was my drinking. It didn't have anything to do with you or Mom. I hurt you, and it's OK to be angry...or sad...or embarrassed. It makes sense that you would be.

The first feeling this father reflects to his son is the boy's humiliation over the episode of the father's public drunkenness. The father's concentration on the child's feelings, his use of some emotion-charged words ("embarrassed" and "awful"), and his permission for the boy to break down release a swell of emotion that the child has probably been suppressing for some time. When the dam finally breaks, it is obvious that it held back much more than the son's feelings of shame about his father's drinking. The anger this boy has been containing reveals itself in his clenched fists and the blows he directs at his knees. However, the son denies the anger when his father reflects it. These sorts of denials should not be taken at face value, but neither is it necessary to wring an explicit acknowledgment of rage from a child in this circumstance. What is important is to note what you saw and to affirm the child's right to feel what you believe he is feeling. This makes it easier for him to express his anger (or his sadness or fear) more directly the next time he is aware of it.

This father has come a long way with his son in the space of what is really a very brief exchange. Of course, this is a hypothetical, and very streamlined, conversation. Still, when a parent focuses intently on a child's emotional state, with a serious and loving determination to understand it, and uses restatement and reflection instead of questions, feelings are released. It may not happen the first, second, or third time you try it. But intense feelings are always pressing for release, and you should eventually make contact. When you do, it will quickly become clear that your child's emotional life is complex. His feelings about most things will be mixed, and you will need some additional tools in order to assist him as he tries to sort things out. *Summarizing* ideas and feelings that a child expresses helps both of you to keep track of what's going on.

Summarization. Summarization is not just for summing up at the end of a conversation. You should use it as soon as you feel things are getting complicated, and you want to: (1) Be sure you understand what your child is trying to say; and/or (2) You want to highlight a thought or emotion that seems to be very important to the child or the situation he is in. When you try to use summaries in conversations with your child, you will naturally feed back to him the themes that struck you as most meaningful. When I summarize with a client, with a friend, or with my own child, I use a very tentative tone, almost as if there were a question mark at the end of my review. I know that when I listen, I may be filtering out thoughts or emotions that are somehow too disturbing for me to let in, or ignoring ideas that are irrelevant in my own scheme of things, but which are terribly important to the other person. I don't use an emphatic, declarative tone, because I don't want to imply that what I heard is definitely what was said, or that it reflects what should have been said. I want to leave lots of room for the speaker to correct my impression.

Our hypothetical father and son have covered a lot of important territory. The father can't help but have his own powerful reactions to this discussion, and it is probably a good time for him to try and review what's gone on, to see if he's remained centered on his son's experience or if his own emotions have colored his view of what his child is saying.

CHILD: I'm OK now Dad. Billy just really gets me upset.

DAD: I know you're upset about the problem with Billy, but it seems to me there are a lot of other things that are bothering you right now, too.

CHILD: I guess.

DAD: Let's see, first, there is Billy. He's really giving you a hard time and making you feel embarrassed and ashamed about my drinking. That's one problem.

CHILD: Yeah.

DAD: The other thing that's bothering you, I think, is that you remember how bad it felt when I was drinking. All the problems we had. And I think when you remember the things I did, you start to feel angry about them.

CHILD: (Nods.) But I shouldn't be. Mom told me you couldn't help it. You were sick.

DAD: Yeah, but the things I did hurt you whether I could help it or not. Anybody would feel angry in your shoes.

CHILD: (Doesn't speak, but stares at the floor.)

DAD: It looks like something's still bothering you.

CHILD: You're really better now, aren't you Dad? Billy's wrong isn't he?

DAD: That's really on your mind, too. Worrying I might drink again.

CHILD: (Nods again.)

DAD: Well, I am better. Right now I don't feel like drinking. But people who are sick can have setbacks. That's why I'm taking good care of myself. I get a lot of help from the meetings I go to, and I'm going to keep going to them. If I should drink again, Mom and I and a lot of other people will know I'm in trouble, and we'll make sure that I get more help, and stop quickly. I just don't think it will be like it was before I went into the hospital. (Pauses.) Any questions?

CHILD: No.

DAD: Why don't you tell me what you heard me say?

CHILD: You could get sick again.

DAD: But I'm getting a lot of help to stay well.

CHILD: The meetings really help.

DAD: And you can ask me about this again, whenever you feel worried. OK?

CHILD: OK.

DAD: Now, let's talk about how to handle Billy.

The father points out that his son is grappling with at least two major problems. He has to figure out a way to handle the taunts from his friend, Billy, and he has to find some way to manage his anger at his father as well. Dad once again affirms the legitimacy of his child's anger. He will have to do this many, many more times before it sticks. The boy agrees that both of these issues are of concern, and then mentions the other great worry he's expressed: Will Dad drink again? The father left this problem out of his summary, perhaps because it is a question that worries him as well, and he isn't quite sure how to respond. His son might have interpreted the omission to mean that Dad was unwilling or unable to discuss the possibility of a relapse, but Dad compensated for the error by picking up on his son's nonverbal cues and reflecting the fact that the boy still seemed troubled. This indicated the father's willingness to keep talking, and provided the child with the encouragement he needed to raise this sensitive topic one more time. Even if a child's nonverbal behavior doesn't tip you to the possibility that there any issues hanging fire after you summarize, it's still a good idea to ask, "So, let's see, did I leave anything out?"

Another useful thing this father did was to ask his son to summarize the things the father had said about his drinking and the possibility that he might relapse. When you and your child are in the thick of a tense, emotional discussion, he is as likely to misconstrue your remarks as you are his. He does not intentionally distort what you are trying to say. However, like you, he has his own needs and feelings and his own sense of what is important. All of these factors influence what he emphasizes and de-emphasizes when he is listening to you. In the preceeding example, the son was so focused on the idea that his father might relapse that he tuned out the more hopeful part of the father's message. If you can teach your child to summarize and feed back what he has heard you say, it will reduce another potential source of misunderstanding between you.

Most people find that it feels artificial and a little silly when they begin to employ active listening skills in conversations with colleagues, or friends, or children. As a first year graduate student, I felt silly when I used these techniques, and I was certain that they were a dead giveaway for my inexperience. I was stunned when during one of my first few interviews with an actual client, she leaned toward me and said, "You know. I like it when you repeat the things I say. I feel like you're really listening to me."

The fact is, that our perception of what other people are trying to communicate is so deeply affected by what we expect to hear, or what we want to hear, or what we are terrified we will hear, that it is a virtual certainty that we will miss or distort great chunks of important information in almost every conversation we have. Active listening skills are the best tools we have for minimizing the possibility of a major breakdown in communication with children and gradually establishing a reliable empathic connection with them.

Beyond Active Listening

Taking Time with Your Children. It takes time and practice to become skilled at the use of restatement, reflection, and summarization. But time is your greatest ally as you pursue greater emotional intimacy with your child. Time with your child is what you need to become familiar with his emotional cycles—his customary reactions to the highs and lows of everyday life. Your frequent companionship, even in the smallest, most mundane moments of everyday life, is what he needs to feel safe again, and reassured of his importance to you. "Quality" time spent together is great for everybody. Trips to the zoo, walks in the park, stories told and read at bedtime are all things that bring you closer together. But it is important to realize that *all* the time you spend together has the potential to improve your child's quality of life, as well as the quality of his self-image and the quality of your relationship with him. For example, sitting with a child as he does his algebra homework can be both soothing and heartening to him. This is true even if you are hopeless at math and even if you are occupied with some task of your own. Remember how lonely it could feel in the library when you were all alone with a big assignment? And how much better it felt to study with a friend? Sometimes all it takes to feel supported is a buddy with enough time and interest to look up from her own work, inquire after your progress, and admire your hard effort. You're suddenly reminded that you're not all alone in the world. Someone cares and will probably still care even if you blow this assignment. This feeling of unconditional love and interest is exactly what you want to communicate to your child. There are many small opportunities in the course of a day to get the message across. With a toddler, a simple routine like bath time will be very important if it is a chance for him to have you all to himself, to engage you in a water game of his own invention and to bask in your playful attention to the wonder of his fingers and toes. The idea is to spare whatever time you can, find a way to watch and listen, and let your child know you're thinking of him. If you do, he'll feel more connected to you and far more secure and self-confident.

Providing Positive Attention. Once again, the emphasis during time with your child should be on *positive* attention. Parents are often tempted to accentuate the negative with a child, especially if he seems stubborn and indifferent to their authority. But children are most likely to act tough and feign indifference when they feel, and are, particularly vulnerable. Harsh reprimands and critical judgments *are* heard, even though a child seems to ignore you, and angry, disapproving evaluations of his character *are* incorporated into his image of himself. No matter what your child says, and how he behaves toward you, it is (and in some ways, always will be) *your* opinion that matters the most to him. In order to be fully responsive to your child's emotional needs, you must be able to recognize and applaud his personal strengths. And you must pay particular attention to those strengths that are the most important to him.

It may be that you've been so immersed in your struggle to stop drinking, or to cope with your spouse's alcoholism that you've lost touch with the qualities, interests, and talents that make your son or daughter truly special. As you think about your relationships with your children, ask yourself if you've fallen into the pattern of disregarding a "good" child who seems to get along with little attention and guidance, or one of constantly scolding and punishing a "troublemaker." Then think about the compliments you do give your children. Do you talk about the merit badges your child worked so hard for in Scouting, or do you tend to emphasize his helpfulness at home, because you need his help so badly? If your answers to these questions trouble you, you can take steps to increase the amount of praise you give your child, and perhaps, begin to change the nature of that praise. First, though, you will have to spend some time watching your child at work and play, and observe his interactions with other people, as well as with you.

If your child is in school, you can begin by talking with his teachers. You want to know about the quality of his schoolwork, certainly, but his teachers will also have information about who his best friends are and what his particular interests and pleasures seem to be. You can also watch your child when he is at play with his chums. What strengths do you feel he brings to his interactions with friends? What qualities do they seem to value in him?

When your child is at home with you and your spouse and his siblings, watch how he spends his time. What are his special toys, his beloved games? How is he progressing with these? Have his block towers become more stable than the last time you looked? Has he learned not to giggle and give away his position when he plays hide and seek? Don't discount these small gains when you consider your child's strengths. Most of us progress in small steps rather than giant leaps.

Now, when you tell your child what's great about him, include the things that matter most to him. He'll be far prouder of making it to the eighth level of his favorite video game than he will be about organizing his closet. Though it's fine to give a nod of approval to achievements that make your life easier, it's also crucial that you respond to your child's emotional agenda. When you speak to the matters that concern him the most, you let him know that he is important for something more than his ability to please or support his parents. You are saying that who he is *as an individual* matters greatly and deeply pleases you.

Providing Physical Attention. Sometimes being in tune with your child involves actual physical touching. Affectionate physical touch is something we all need, because it is a tangible expression of the love and connection with others that we crave. Alcoholism and the wall of denial that rises around it create a painful emotional distance between family members. Hugs, kisses, cuddling, and the joining of hands create a physical bridge across the gulf of disappointments and misunderstandings that separate you. They confer a feeling of security that is often essential in soothing a child who feels panicked, angry, or terribly sad.

Physical touch can be extremely problematic for adults who grew up in families that were afraid of, or opposed to, physical displays of affection. It can also be terribly disturbing to people who were physically or sexually abused as children. If the prospect of touching your child feels frightening to you, this is an important matter to take up with a professional helper.

A parent's loving touch provides a child with tangible evidence of his unique value. When a child is touched with tenderness, he understands that he is capable of inspiring warm and loving feelings in another person. All children and all adults long to feel lovable to other people. And everyone measures their worth, to some extent, by others' readiness to come physically close to them. Your child will sense any fear that you feel about touching him, and he will conclude that there is something bad or ugly about him that repulses you. If you are afraid you'll hurt your child if you allow yourself to get too close, then, of course, don't touch him. But do get professional help with this problem right away, and explain to your child that whereas hugging and holding hands is great when people love each other, problems in your past make these behaviors uncomfortable for you. Emphasize that the problem is yours, and that there is nothing wrong with him, or the physical contact he wants. A child should never be told that his desire for cuddling, kissing, or hugging is "babyish" or "bad." It is normal and healthy to want physical contact with others, and you must reassure your child of this.

The type and amount of physical contact a child desires will change as he grows older. Babies and toddlers need a great amount of contact, especially holding and cuddling. They are building a fundamental feeling of security and value to see them through their entire life cycle, and they don't yet have a facility with language to help them establish this strong base. As children grow older, they are better able to process and use loving words to help them build self-esteem, and touching becomes somewhat less important (though never unimportant). Furthermore, the older children get, the more concerned they are with issues of independence and self-determination. They still want hugs and kisses, but they want them on their own terms and in their own time. When a child enters puberty, he has to deal with the pressure of his sexual impulses and cope with compelling emotional needs as well. At this point, the issue of self-management becomes intensely important and the youngster must feel that he is in complete control of his body.

Your general guideline in gauging the amount and kind of physical contact to provide your child should be to try and meet his demonstrated need. If you bend over to kiss your child on the head while he's reading and he says, "Hey, not now! I'm concentrating!" try not to dwell on the rejecting quality of his response. Instead, reflect on the idea that he believes his feelings and boundaries are important, and that he seems to think that he can get you to respect them. This is a very important developmental achievement. As the next section of this chapter makes clear, this is an achievement that can be hard to come by in an alcoholic family.

You have an innate need for contact comfort just as your child does, but you must find other grown-ups to ensure that you get the physical closeness you need. Your child's personal needs about the issue of touching must always take precedence over yours. In fact, as a general rule, in recovering families, any errors about limits should be made on the side of preserving the child's physical and psychological boundaries.

Observing Psychological Boundaries. When professional helpers speak of a person's psychological boundaries, they are referring to the set of internal rules the individual uses to make decisions about how hard he will work to meet his own needs versus how hard he will try to supply what someone else needs. Children in alcoholic families often find it difficult to establish and maintain reasonable psychological boundaries. If your child has a hard time setting limits, then you, as a therapeutic, and emotionally responsive parent, will need to help him become more cognizant and respectful of his own feelings. Your attempt to be sensitive to his needs will be most helpful to him in this regard.

In the best of situations, children have only the most limited sort of control over their lives. What control they do have depends on their ability to communicate their needs to their parents and to evoke in them the wish to help satisfy these needs. When parents exhibit a reasonable amount of sensitivity to a child's emotional needs, the child develops a respect for his own feelings that enables him to go into the world and try to get his most important needs met. Further, since others respect his feelings, he is inclined to have an attitude of respect for the feelings and needs of his friends and acquaintances. With some practice, he develops a facility for finding compromises when his needs conflict with those of others.

When a preoccupation with alcohol prevents parents from sensing and responding to children's needs, the children experience a terrifying sense of impotence and vulnerability. Some youngsters in this situation become overly passive and receptive to the chaotic environment in which they live. Their philosophy seems to be, "Go with the flow. Give the big people what they need and don't want or ask for anything because you'll end up getting disappointed." Other kids who feel unbearably vulnerable become obsessed with acquiring some kind of control over their lives. All children need to feel a degree of self-control, but children in alcoholic families may compensate for feelings of powerlessness by insisting on very rigid physical or emotional boundaries. This child feels, "I can't do anything about them. But I will control me." Both strategies aim at ensuring psychic survival in a chaotic situation, but each one exposes the child to peril if it is carried to an extreme. The overly compliant child may avoid physical punishment when his parents are out of control, but he can be easily exploited, because he doesn't feel it is possible to say no to even the most outrageous demand. This kind of child is particularly vulnerable to sexual abuse. The youngster who concentrates intensely and narrowly on controlling his body or his mind feels less panicky and less vulnerable about the chaos around him, but may become so obsessed with his internal world that he fails to develop skills for adapting to and dealing with other people. He is also a candidate for compulsive problems, including eating disorders.

Children who are unable to set up balanced and reasonable personal boundaries usually need professional assistance (See chapters 9 and 10), but they also require particularly careful attention to the issue of limits from therapeutic parents. Neither the compliant child nor the rigid child should be pressured about physical contact (or any other issue pertaining to a parent's emotional need). As therapeutic parents, you are, as always, concerned about *empowering* your child.

You can help the overly compliant child to define and assert psychological limits by providing opportunities for him to make age-appropriate choices, and by promoting activities that emphasize self-reflection and exploration. This is a child who should have a room, or some place in the home that is all his own. His room should be a place where he makes some of the big decisions about decorations and placement of furniture, where his important things are kept, and are under his control, and where he can go and close the door. If you have a weekly family time when there are choices to be made about a family activity, take turns selecting the activity and make sure this child gets his share of opportunities to call the shots. When you are shopping for new clothes, ask him what he thinks and what his favorite colors are, and allot some portion of the budget for selections that will be entirely his own. (The amount of the clothes budget that is his to control should increase according to his age.)

Older children should actively join in the process of making decisions about elective subjects in school, extracurricular activities to join, and social functions to attend. Parents can teach their children the process of effective decision-making, emphasizing the need to set goals that express personal values and to carefully weigh the pros and cons of alternative courses of action. As children become increasingly able to consider the implications of their actions, and as they demonstrate a willingness and ability to protect their own well-being, and that of others, they should be given greater autonomy.

The child who establishes and protects very rigid personal boundaries will be disinclined to relax them until he is convinced that you, his parents, are back in control of the family and yourselves. When you identify and enforce reasonable limits for family members, and consistently care for the physical and emotional needs of the household, the "overcontrolled" child will begin to let down his guard. Unless he's doing something that could hurt himself or others, don't pressure him to eat more or less than he's determined to eat, don't insist that he change his hairstyle, and don't ask him to relax or heighten his standards for grooming or exercise. Try to see and respect his behaviors for what they are—legitimate attempts to establish control at a time when the world around him is spinning dangerously out of control. You might even say, "You want to be the boss of things that are important to you. Everybody feels this way." If you feel you must fight over some issue with him, pick it carefully. Try to lay back where matters of individual preference are concerned, and oppose him only in matters that are a significant threat to his physical or emotional well-being and safety. Meanwhile, be rigid and scrupulous yourself about keeping promises and strive to fulfill your own resolutions concerning your program of recovery. This, more than anything, will help your overcontrolled child to relax, and to allow his boundaries to become more flexible.

Emotional Responsiveness versus Emotional Indulgence

Guilt and the wish to make up for lost time may lead some recovering parents to confuse emotional responsiveness with emotional and material indulgence. As you get better and stronger, you will be less absorbed by your own struggle and better able to appreciate how hurt your children feel and how disappointed in you they truly are. This will naturally arouse in you the fervent wish to compensate for them their suffering.

Your children may actually believe that their pain will dissolve if they acquire enough toys and clothes and electronic gadgets. Many children from alcoholic homes, who have been deprived of appropriate and adequate emotional care, become compulsive shoppers in their effort to fill the internal void created by long years of family illness and conflict. However, whereas your children may press and beg you for things, what they really crave is your time and your willingness to share your emotional world with them. Even though they may bully and berate you, they deeply long for your devoted attention to their feelings and needs.

It will be particularly hard for you to concentrate on the emotional bottom line—your youngsters' need for empathy, intimacy, and reasonable limits—if they are very angry, accusing, and demanding. The difficulty is compounded if your own parents were insensitive to your need for love and understanding. However, your family situation can never improve if you surrender to your children's outrageous material demands or indulge their wish to avenge the past by tormenting you. Your capitulation to their agitated demands and accusations will only provoke further tantrums and tirades. You and your children will only find peace through your sustained, consistent, and determined efforts to understand how they feel. You might review the case of Paul's family (chapter 5), as well as the next story, which concerns a mother's dedicated effort to remain empathic with her child, while also resisting emotional abuse from her.

NATALIE

I left my husband because he was drinking all the time, dealing crack, and selling all our possessions to support his own habit. The problem is, I didn't leave soon enough. I took all the cruelty and abuse until my daughter—well, I guess she figured I'd never get on top of things, and she'd never be able to count on me. She had to believe in somebody, so she came to the conclusion that I was causing all the trouble in the family and that her father was just fine. When I finally left, and sued for custody, she was furious at me for breaking up the family. The first time she asked me why I did it, I told her it was because of what her father was doing, and that I felt all our lives were in danger. Even though she had seen just about everything I had seen in that apartment, she put her hands over her ears and screamed at me that I was a liar. So I understood that she isn't able to face the truth yet. I stopped saying anything against her father, because it only made her hate me and push me away more. She couldn't trust me for such a long time, so now she has to believe he's a good, loving father who will take care of her. It hurts so much when she tells me how cruel I am, and how I'm ruining her life by keeping her from him. She's even tried to slap me, and I won't allow that, or any cursing or name-calling. But I listen when she tells me how I've hurt her, and I tell her I know that's true, but I'm trying to do the right thing now. Lots of times I want to scream back at her, and tell her how unfair this all is. I risked my life to get her away from the needles, and guns and derelicts and criminals that were all over our place. But my therapist and my sister helped me to understand—I've got to let her feel what she feels right now. She's testing me. Am I really stronger now? Or will I hurt her when she pushes me too hard? Will I rant and rave at her like I used to? Will I run away? Or will I stay on my feet and give her the love she needs? I really just want to be her mother again. But it seems like it will be a long time before she's willing to give me that chance.

Conclusion

Some children from alcoholic families feel unloved, unimportant, and emotionally isolated all their lives. It is not the fact of a parent's addiction that undoes a child. It is the fact that the addiction results in the parent's emotional abandonment of him that proves utterly destructive to a youngster's hope and sense of self-worth.

Parental abstinence from drinking, drugging, and enabling behaviors creates an opportunity for new and dramatic emotional growth in children. Most of these changes, when they occur, are the result of parents' increased ability to empathize with and emotionally support their children.

The emotional needs of children in recovery are powerful and complex. These children are frightened, sad, and lonely. They are also angry. It requires great courage, as well as ample support from helpers outside the family, for parents to face these emotions with their children. The willingness to confront your child's pain, even when you understand that you are the source of his injury, is the greatest gift you can offer your child. It will be the most powerful force for recovery in his life.

BEING EMOTIONALLY RESPONSIVE TO YOUR CHILD

- Assign feelings and needs a high priority in your home
- Manage conflict with the rules of fair fighting
- Model self-respect and self-care
- Use active listening techniques
    - Restatement
    - Reflection
    - Summarization
- Take time with your children
- Provide positive attention
- Treat your child as an individual
- Provide physical affection
- Observe your child's physical and emotional boundaries
- Respond, don't indulge

= 8 =

Protecting Your Children's Physical Security

Physical security is a child's most fundamental right and most fundamental need. When physical security is threatened, every other aspect of a child's functioning is jeopardized as well. Health, intellectual development, and emotional and psychological growth are all derailed when a child is exposed to chronic sexual or other physical abuse, or when he is repeatedly endangered or neglected by the adults he loves and depends upon. The danger and the damage are compounded when one parent is abusive, and the other parent does not intervene to protect the child. Children who are abused on the one hand, and emotionally abandoned on the other, exist on a plane of torment and despair unknown and unknowable to most of us. Most are permanently scarred by this experience, and many find that the profound feelings of betrayal and distrust engendered by their childhood experience complicate and confound their efforts to find love and comfort in adult relationships.

Abusive and nonprotective parents are usually too ill to acknowledge their actions and their destructiveness, or to exercise control over their own behavior. Even when they are in treatment, it is often a very long time before the shameful, painful secret of their abusive behavior is revealed. *It is usually up to the nonabusive parent to take action when physical abuse is occurring in the home. If you suspect that your child is being abused, neglected, or endangered, you must take whatever steps are necessary to protect him.*

The aim of this chapter is to help you recognize threats to your children's physical security, and to help you act in a timely and effective way to eliminate these threats. The next section specifies the steps that must be taken if your child's security is threatened because the family is in severe economic straits, and you're afraid that you won't be able to provide adequate food, clothing, or shelter. Subsequent sections describe

116

what you must do if your child is being physically abused, physically neglected, or physically endangered by an impaired parent.

When the Family is Economically Threatened

When a parent's drinking and drugging jeopardizes the family's economic security, adults in the family naturally feel anxious and depressed. When parents become anxious and obviously unhappy, this inflames a child's concern for his own situation. If you are worried about providing for your children and keeping a roof over their heads, it is too much to ask that you set your anxiety aside. And it is not a good idea for you to mask your concern in an effort to induce a false sense of security in your children. First of all, most children develop an acute sensitivity to their parents' emotional states. They may pretend to be misled by a charade of confidence and cheer, but inside they know something is wrong. They set their imaginations to work in an effort to divine the cause of father and mother's anxiety, and are very likely to conjure a worse scenario than that which actually threatens the family. Second, as explained in chapter 5, emotional dishonesty is incompatible with the goal of creating a therapeutic atmosphere in the home.

If you are plagued with financial anxiety, and you wish to remain in a therapeutic posture with your children, your only viable option is to do something to restore your own confidence. Most children can tolerate a mood of urgency and struggle in a parent as long as they sense that he is still looking for solutions and is determined to find one that works for the family. In other words, it is restorative to children when a parent regains hope and strives to take charge of a deteriorating situation. You will begin to regain hope and to rebuild confidence when you begin to take action of some kind. The most immediately rewarding and inspirational action you can take, if your home and your livelihood are endangered is to share your sense of danger and desperation with constructive friends and helpers outside the family. The very act of sharing a heavy emotional burden tends to reduce it and to stimulate the process of active problem solving as well. People outside the family are in a position to offer emotional support, which is essential if you are to overcome the kind of paralysis that sets in when you are terribly afraid and feeling ashamed and hopeless as well. Furthermore, they can provide a perspective on the problem and generate ideas that are not distorted by feelings of guilt and responsibility for the problem itself, or by the need to stabilize their own imperiled self-esteem. Finally, they can help to identify and gather the type of information you'll need in order to take further effective action, including information about legal aid, housing, and financial counseling. If you have a supportive, compassionate friend who is able to think clearly when presented with a crisis, you can start by speaking with her. If you don't have such a friend, then you should consult a professional helper as soon as possible. See chapter 10, which describes strategies for choosing an appropriate counselor.

If you do not find an outlet for the expression of your worst fears and continue to struggle with them in near-complete isolation, you will almost certainly find that they become more intense, more disturbing, and more difficult to manage. If you fail to confide in another adult who is willing to help you discuss, explore, and resolve your fears, you may begin to transmit them to your children. In your frustration and despair, you may begin to lash out at your kids as well.

On the other hand, if you can voice your desperation to a helpful friend, sponsor, or mental health professional and begin to see yourself moving, however gradually, toward a solution, you will be able to present a genuinely positive and confident face to your children. Of course, your fears will not vanish overnight, and there will still be times when you feel hopeless and defeated. But your children will perceive your growth and your progress. They will feel heartened when they see that you are able to move forward in spite of your fear, and they will be inspired to persevere in their own struggle for continued growth.

It is vital that you avoid making your children confidantes or counselors when you feel overwhelmed with pain and fear about the future. Again, children will, in most cases, tolerate a parent's anxiety without losing their own hope and feeling of security. However, their sense of security will erode and eventually collapse under the pressure of a parent's desperation, and it is a desperate parent indeed who turns to a child for marital or financial advice.

When There Is Physical Abuse

You must take immediate and dramatic action when a child is being subjected to physical abuse, including sexual abuse.

The emotional and psychological climate in the alcoholic family is conducive to a pattern of physical and sexual abuse. This is not because alcoholic and codependent parents are bad, immoral people. It is because normal inhibitions against violence are reduced under the influence of alcohol, because alcoholic families tend to be emotionally and socially isolated, and because members of these families experience chronic and intense stress.

Each person in a disintegrating alcoholic family feels responsible for the chaos and pain that surrounds him. When people feel responsible for trouble, they also feel deeply ashamed of themselves. As we have seen, this leads both alcoholic and codependent family members to devote a considerable amount of time and energy to concealing and compensating for the drinking problem, as well as the complications that have arisen from it. As the family grows increasingly isolated and increasingly troubled, each member begins to stagger and bend beneath the weight of his or her own bad feelings. None of them can manage this burden indefinitely. Those who do not reduce it by expressing their distress to a constructive friend or helper will often turn to a compulsion of some sort in an effort to quiet their inner torment.

Either the alcoholic or the codependent parent may become compulsively violent as a means of overcoming chronic feelings of powerlessness, shame, and victimization. Further, since the family has become so practiced at hiding and denying its misery, and because it has isolated itself from outside observation and influence, a parent may be able to dismiss even the most obvious evidence of violence against his children, thereby allowing it to continue and to escalate. Some parents actually witness acts of abuse without intervening to protect a child. They convince themselves that the abuse is not serious or truly harmful to the child. Or, they see it as somehow justified and appropriate in light of the child's behavior. Some parents feel helpless to oppose an abusive spouse.

Children naturally expect parents to protect them and they suffer greatly when this trust is violated. Experts on the problem of childhood abuse point out that, when a child is physically abused by a parent, rather than by a stranger, this actually heightens the traumatic impact of the injury. In fact, some of the most severe and lasting damage to the self of a child occurs when one parent physically/sexually abuses a child and the other parent fails to stop it.

The following sections describe the forms of physical and sexual abuse that children may experience in an alcoholic home, and the measures that a parent must take to stop such abuse. Chapter 9 provides further information about behaviors and problems that are likely to appear when a child is being victimized by a parent. If you suspect that your child is being abused by your spouse, please read this chapter and chapter 10 very carefully, and solicit professional help immediately.

Sexual Abuse of Children

What Is Sexual Abuse? Parents preoccupied by sexual obsessions abuse children in different ways. Some refrain from crossing a physical boundary, but grossly violate crucial psychological boundaries. For example, a parent may torment a child with demands for excessive cleanliness and purity. Some parents thoughtlessly or deliberately expose their children to pornographic media. In one family I counseled, a stepfather took pictures of his stepdaughter in various states of undress. It is also a violation of an important psychological boundary when a parent discusses sexual problems or sexual escapades with his children. All of these acts constitute sexual abuse, even though they do not involve physical contact.

Some parents do cross a physical boundary with their children. They expose themselves, masturbate in front of a child, fondle the child's breasts or genitals, or rape or sodomize a child. Sexual abuse may involve penetration of the child's body, but it may not. Sometimes sexual abuse is conducted violently, and other times it is performed with a degree of tenderness. Whatever the context though, when a child observes or participates in sexual acts with an adult, this is abusive and exploitative.

Family Conditions That May Lead to Sexual Abuse. Several conditions predispose a family to a pattern of sexual exploitation and violence. Sexual abuse of a child by a parent is more likely to occur in those alcoholic homes in which one or both parents is often absent or so incapacitated that a child has assumed many parental functions. A child who takes on much responsibility for the management of the household, such as cooking, cleaning, and caring for siblings, is often exploited sexually as well. If the mother in an alcoholic home was battered and/or sexually abused as a child, and especially if she is now being battered by her husband, she is very likely to feel the deep sense of powerlessness that is so common among people who are chronically victimized. In this case, she may be psychologically unable to help her children define appropriate boundaries and may feel helpless to impose such boundaries on her compulsive and abusive husband. This heightens the possibility that her children will be abused.

The odds that sexual abuse will occur are also increased in families in which there is little appropriate physical expression of tenderness and love; little snuggling, hugging, or age-appropriate caressing. Children crave this kind of contact-comfort, and seem to be especially vulnerable to sexual exploitation if it is presented and performed with a display of tenderness that represents their only source of "loving" physical contact with another human being.

Chronic emotional abuse of children, especially shaming and humiliation, creates a feeling of worthlessness and a sense that further abuse, including sexual violation, is justified.

Finally, children who have been taught that family secrets must be kept at all costs, that any anguish and torment must be concealed, and that no one outside the family is to be trusted, are more likely to be victimized and for a longer period.

Children Never Consent to Sexual Abuse. It is critical for parents to understand that a child is unable to consent to sexual activity with an adult. A child has neither the psychological maturity nor the real freedom to offer full and informed consent to such activity. A child may submit to sexual pressure from an adult, without any apparent complaint, because she misunderstands her responsibility to him, or is desperate to win his love, or because she fears him, but this does not, by any stretch of the imagination, amount to consent.

Parents should also realize that, as specialists in the field of sexual abuse advise us, sexual victimization is a sexual means of establishing domination and control over another, less powerful human being. It is fundamentally an act of aggression, and an attempt to discharge one's own feeling of vulnerability and victimization into another person. Once a pattern of failing self-esteem and compensatory aggression and exploitation is established in a family, it tends to escalate in frequency and intensity as time goes on.

When to Suspect Sexual Abuse. Chapter 9 describes in detail behaviors and physical and psychological maladies that are often associated with sexual abuse (See chapter 9, *Reactions to Traumatic Stress.*)

A sexually abused child may be extremely withdrawn and fearful, socially isolated, and passive, and depressed in manner. On the other hand, some sexually abused children appear to be very anxious, and some are extremely aggressive in their social behavior. An abused child may be hostile or make inappropriate sexual gestures toward other children. Older children are often truant, as well as delinquent, and many run away from home to escape the abuse. Sexually abused children often develop compulsive disorders, including compulsive overeating and drug abuse, in order to manage the anxiety and hurt they feel. Some children appear to show no ill effects at all. They are industrious, helpful, orderly, and cooperative. Every bit of their pain seems to be submerged. *All chronically abused children, regardless of their behavioral response to the sexual exploitation they are experiencing, suffer from critically low self-esteem.* Some attempt suicide when they conclude that there is no other avenue of escape from the pain they feel.

Many Abused Children Try to Report Abuse. Many children approach a nonabusive parent directly about sexual abuse by the other parent. They may not have the verbal facility to fully describe what has happened to them, but do talk about "bad touching" or play that hurt them or made them uncomfortable. A child should always be given the benefit of your belief when she discloses such information. Very few children lie or fantasize about sexual abuse. On the contrary, they are terrified by the abuse, and terrified of what will happen to them, and to the family, if they expose the situation. Usually, they have been threatened by the abusive parent, as a means of securing their silence and submission. When a child rises above her terror to tell the truth, it is essential that her complaint be regarded seriously, and that action be taken as soon as possible to prevent further abuse.

What Action to Take. A child who exhibits any of these signs and symptoms should be taken to a specialist in child psychiatry or psychology immediately. If you cannot afford private treatment, your county Health Department can refer you to state or county-supported programs that offer free, or low cost services. During your initial consultation with the treatment provider, you should ask whether he or she is comfortable and experienced in treating members of alcoholic families (see chapter 10) and families in which there is physical abuse. You should tell the counselor that you are concerned about the possibility that your child has been sexually abused. If the counselor does not respond to your concern by asking questions and discussing the need to report the abuse to the proper authorities, you should ask for another interview with another counselor. To learn more about what happens when you or a professional helper report sexual abuse, read the section in this chapter entitled *When You Report Child Abuse.*

Physical Brutality

It is also imperative that you intervene if your child is being physically beaten by your spouse.

Hitting a child is not an appropriate method of discipline, nor is it an especially effective teaching device. What you do, and who you are as a person, has a dramatic effect on who, and what, your children become. What you say is important to your children, but it has far less influence on their behavior than your actions. When a parent beats a child and tells him that she is trying to teach him to behave decently, the child becomes filled with hurt, frustration, anger, and disappointment. All he really learns from this experience is that it is appropriate to handle powerful feelings of conflict and pain by hurting those who are less powerful than he is. Such a child is very likely to perpetuate the cycle of physical violence he has experienced into the next generation. Nearly all parents who abuse children were abused when they, themselves, were small.

When to Suspect Physical Abuse. In general, you should suspect that your child is being beaten if she frequently has bruises, fractured or broken bones, or repeated injury to the same part of the body. Behavioral and psychological problems often result from chronic physical abuse. The kinds of problems that appear are similar to those described in the discussion of sexual abuse and in the section in chapter 9 concerning

Reactions to Traumatic Stress. Certainly, you should believe your child if he tells you that your spouse is hurting him. What usually happens, however, is that the abusive parent offers a plausible explanation for frequent injuries, and the child, who is afraid of further abuse and afraid of conflict between his parents, supports this explanation. However, you may notice that the explanation does not jibe with the extent of the child's injuries, and that your spouse often fails to get medical help for him in a timely way.

What Action to Take. If you feel any suspicion whatsoever that your child has been physically abused, you must seek professional intervention and investigation. A family or emergency room physician, a child psychiatrist, or a child psychologist can help you determine whether your child's injuries and complaints are consistent with abuse. Medical and mental health professionals, and others who work with children, must report suspected child abuse. The section that follows shortly, entitled When You Report Child Abuse, will help you to understand the procedures that professional helpers and child protection authorities follow in helping families deal with the problem of physical abuse.

Other Physical Abuse

Parents under the influence of chemical intoxicants and chronic stress may physically injure children in other ways, as well.

Physical Neglect and Endangerment. These are both forms of child abuse. The neglected infant or child is often underweight. Sometimes it is obvious to teachers and neighbors that he is not being cared for, because he appears unkempt, unwashed, and is not properly outfitted against harsh weather conditions. He may be ill frequently, and struggling to keep up with other children in physical and academic activities.

Even if a child receives enough good food to eat and is neatly and appropriately dressed, he may still be neglected. A child is neglected if he spends all or part of his day with a parent who is too drunk to function as a parent—who can't help him get meals or ensure his physical welfare and safety in the home; who may leave him to cry in his room (or his crib) because she has passed out on the living room couch.

Alcoholic parents in a state of intoxication and mental confusion often physically endanger children. They drive while drunk, with their helpless children in the car. They smoke and drop lit cigarettes onto the carpet or under the cushions of upholstered furniture. Some are so desperate to maintain a supply of drugs that they allow dealers and other addicts to sell and use drugs in their homes while their minor children are present.

What Action to Take. If your spouse is actively alcoholic, you must never assume that she will be able to control the need to drink or do drugs simply because your child is present and because she loves him and is responsible for his welfare. You must remember the case of Will (chapter 2) and accept the fact that at any given moment the craving for a drink or a drug, may become the sole focus of your spouse's attention. If this happens, she will become bent on satisfying this craving and will completely forget her responsibility toward the children. This can happen even if she is a perfectly adequate parent when sober, and even though she deeply loves her children. An active alcoholic, who is not in a formal program of recovery and who has not established a stable sobriety, should not be left to care alone for minor children.

It is not appropriate, and it is not sufficient, to give an older child the ongoing responsibility of playing "watchdog" over an alcoholic parent and younger siblings. There must be a sober, responsible adult present at all times, who is capable of intervening to protect your children if your spouse begins to drink.

When You Report Child Abuse

It is always frightening for members of alcoholic families to expose their family crisis to outsiders. They fear they will be blamed, shamed, and condemned for the alcoholism, and for the chaos it has created. They also fear that if they report the possibility that their children are being abused, the children will be taken away from them.

Alcoholism is still poorly understood by many professionals, and many lay people continue to regard alcoholism as a moral lapse. However, today, a great many medical and mental health professionals are well schooled, and highly experienced in the treatment of alcoholism and codependence. Addictions specialists are well aware of the high incidence of physical abuse and neglect in alcoholic families, and they will be prepared to refer you and your child to a competent practitioner of child analysis or psychotherapy, as well as to social service authorities who can legally ensure that your child will be protected.

You should be aware that medical and mental health professionals and other professionals who work with children have a legal obligation to report suspected child abuse to a state or county authority that is charged with the protection of children. Usually, this authority will send a social worker to interview you and your child and your spouse to determine whether abuse is actually occurring, and what actions must be taken to stop it. The goal of this investigation is not to punish the abusive parent or to separate you or your spouse from your children.

Child protection authorities recognize that removing a child from his home often subjects him to additional, significant trauma. This step will be taken only if it is necessary to protect the child's security, and it is usually intended as a temporary solution. The principal aim of social service authorities, when they intervene in cases of suspected child abuse, is to support the endangered child and to prevent the recurrence of abuse. Most often, this is accomplished by requiring that parents and children in the home receive extensive counseling.

In treatment, children are helped to express the grief and anger they feel about the abuse that has occurred, and parents are helped to identify and solve the psychological, emotional, and environmental problems that lead to the abuse. Parental alcoholism should be diagnosed during the course of the investigation by social services or during subsequent counseling. When it is, an appropriate, affordable referral will be made to a substance abuse treatment program.

Conclusion

The foundation for a child's feeling of security is his sense of physical safety. He must believe that he will be adequately housed and fed, and that he will be protected from others who mean him harm. When parents find themselves in severe emotional and financial straits on account of drinking or drugging, it may become difficult to provide these basic elements of survival.

The first step to take when you are seeking to break a cycle of physical insecurity, neglect, endangerment, or abuse is to talk to a helper outside the immediate family. *Emotional and social isolation are great enemies of change and enormous obstacles to family recovery.*

Choose a helper whom you know to be compassionate and nonjudgmental. Choose someone who will honor your need for privacy, but avoid those who have a stake in denying or concealing your family's distress. Parents, in-laws, or siblings cannot be helpful confidantes if they tend to become so anxious or embarrassed when the family is in trouble that they sweep problems under the rug.

Where there is a real possibility that your child is being physically abused, you must secure professional help as soon as possible. Your child has been hurt, psychologically as well as physically, and she will need sophisticated and informed assistance in order to recover from her injuries. She may need some medical intervention.

It is never easy to reveal the problem of child abuse to outsiders. You will feel terribly afraid when you take this step. You must try to remember that a competent professional will have the same goal you do—to protect your child. This helper will know that your child's long-term interests are best protected by healing, and strengthening the family, and she will work toward this end. You must also remember that although the process of recovery and growth is very painful at times, the alternative to change is severe and lasting damage to your child.

≡ 9 ≡

The Child Who Needs
Professional Assessment

Some children respond extremely well to stress even when it is relatively intense and prolonged. These resilient children are sometimes called "invulnerables" by sociologists and mental health professionals. Even in the harshest of personal circumstances, they are able to maintain an optimistic outlook, as well as a capacity for achievement and rewarding relatedness with others. And they seem able to do so with the most minimal sort of adult support and guidance.

Some of these invulnerable children will, no doubt, develop problems in later life; some will not. Perhaps truly resilient children are possessed of a naturally sunny temperament and a naturally strong constitution. Undoubtedly, many such children also receive solid support during their infancy and early childhood, as well as at crucial developmental junctures. Most people tolerate stress more easily when they have already acquired a firm sense of self and strong and stable self-esteem.

Children who do not receive strong early support, who are constitutionally more vulnerable to stress, or who are challenged at transitional points in their psychological and emotional development are more likely to break down under the pressure of parental alcoholism or to establish dysfunctional patterns of handling the stress they are experiencing at home. Some other factors that increase the risk of serious behavioral or emotional problems in children of alcoholic and codependent parents include

- Significant, and chronic economic stress in the household
- Chronic illness in both parents
  - Alcoholism or other chemical dependence in both parents
  - A mental illness in the sober parent or
  - A disabling physical illness in the sober parent
- Profound emotional and social isolation as a result of the geographic or psychological circumstances of the family
- Chronic physical disability or illness in the child
- Sexual and/or other physical abuse

In general, then, it is the child who is exposed to extreme or multiple stressors who is most likely to need professional assistance when he is challenged by parental alcoholism and codependence. This chapter provides some guidelines for determining whether professional assessment is indicated for your child. It describes behaviors that are indicative of healthy functioning in children and contrasts these with symptoms that reflect a breakdown in a child's ability to cope constructively with daily life and pressures at home. It provides information about problems that may arise in very young children, as well as syndromes that can develop in older youngsters. The guidelines presented here are intended to alert you to potential problems in development and adjustment. They will not enable you to diagnose specific disorders, and they are not a substitute for formal assessment by a mental health professional.

The Healthy Child

Psychological health is only partly defined by the absence of emotional illness and dysfunctional coping patterns that are described later in this chapter. Psychological health also includes many positive attributes and skills.

In younger children, who have no, or only rudimentary, verbal skills, and little opportunity to establish relationships outside the immediate family, emotional health is usually measured by the strength and quality of attachment the child displays within his family group, especially with his mother or other primary caretaker. A capacity for attachment usually appears by about seven to nine months of age. The child who is bonding normally to his parents stays close to them, but is also brave enough to explore his surroundings insofar as he is physically able to do so. He becomes upset when "his" adults leave, and is considerably cheered when they return. He is able to be comforted, most of the time, by the adults he is close to and to make age-appropriate gains in physical and intellectual development. (The Gesell series on child development is a helpful guide to age-appropriate behavior and developmental gains. See the Suggested Reading section at the end of this book.)

Emotional and psychological health is assessed in more diverse and complex ways as children's verbal and physical skills mature. As children grow, they are able to make more satisfying use of native gifts in their play and in their work at school. They are increasingly able to identify and express significant aspects of their emotional experience at appropriate times when there are supportive peers or adults at hand to receive these communications. The child with normal levels of self-esteem and healthy faith in the goodwill of other people becomes better able to ask for support, assistance, and advice as time goes on. He sometimes turns to people in his family for this help, but he also has relationships with people outside the family on which he can rely.

The healthy child also solves a greater variety of problems on his own as he grows older. He recognizes more easily that he is in a bind, and he is quicker to activate creative processes within himself to work through his dilemma.

Emotional Self-Regulation and Self-Expression

Adults sometimes assume that because children are physically small, their feelings are not as strong and compelling as those that adults experience. However, young children have very vivid and powerful emotional experiences. It is their psychological defenses and controls that are modest and relatively undeveloped, so that they are actually more likely to be overwhelmed by psychological trauma and even the ups and downs of daily life, than is the average adult.

The ability to regulate emotional experience is a cornerstone of psychological health. However, it takes time, as well as adult support and guidance, for children to develop some measure of control over their powerful affects. Most children feel a strong impulse to act directly or to withdraw from the field when they are seized by a strong feeling. Even an older child will shut down, or "lose it," from time to time, given the right combination of physical, emotional, and environmental pressures. But, as time goes on, a healthy child is better able to stand his ground, and to pull his punches when he does lash out physically or verbally. He is usually able to use words, rather than actions, to express what is happening to him internally.

It is very important not to confuse self-regulation with the absolute suppression of strong or negative emotions. Some parents feel that in order to teach their children self-control, they must stress the importance of keeping a stiff upper lip and the value of remaining cooperative and uncomplaining in all circumstances. This antipathy to feelings seems to be particularly entrenched in families in which alcoholism and other drug dependencies have been transmitted through several generations. It is as though the pressure placed on generations of children to keep the shameful family secret, and to become prematurely self-reliant, has destroyed everyone's belief in, and capacity for, emotional awareness and self-expression.

Emotional self-regulation is not about suppressing important and compelling feelings. It is about the ability and the willingness to talk through rather than "act out" emotional experience. This is a capacity that evolves gradually in children, and it is tied to the development of speech and language skills. It is also tied to parents' understanding and acceptance of the human need to communicate powerful emotion.

Aggression versus Self-Assertion. Parents are usually particularly concerned about angry and aggressive behavior in their children. It is important to be alert to problems that develop in this area, but it is also important to understand that anger is a normal reaction to being hurt or thwarted, and children must have some means of releasing and working through angry feelings. For this reason, parents must make a distinction between behavior that is truly aggressive and that which is self-assertive. The principal goal of aggressive behavior, whether it is verbal or physical in form, is to hurt, to humiliate, to dominate another person. Self-assertive behavior, on the other hand, is fundamentally an attempt, however clumsily executed, to express, in words (or in pre-verbal children, through actions), an important need or feeling.

Confusion often arises because self-assertive behavior may include the expression of feelings that disappoint others or inflict emotional pain. Furthermore, the wish to inflict pain is sometimes a secondary goal of self-assertive behavior. For example, the child whose efforts to play with his sister are spurned might scream, "You make me so angry—I hate you!" at his sister, and then run to his room and slam the door. He undoubtedly hopes that his angry withdrawal will leave his sister feeling as bad about the situation as he does. But he has made some effort to describe his own inner state to his sister, and he has taken some care (either deliberately or unconsciously) to avoid alienating her in the extreme. He did not assassinate her character, attack her physically, or take something precious from her. Therefore, the door is left open to the possibility of a later, more meaningful emotional exchange with her. The rift between the two is likely to be repaired. There is even a chance that the relationship can be strengthened if the two can continue to talk about their feelings with each other. (Conflict always has this hopeful aspect. When the opposing parties can stay on the scene and keep talking, there is the opportunity for each to know the other and to be known more deeply.)

Another child might smash his sister's toy when she excludes him from her game. This child is also sending signals about his internal pain, but he is more strongly compelled to transmit this pain than the first child. His actions are far more aggressive in that they are more assaultive and destructive of the bond with his sibling, and they are more likely to arouse a desire for vengeance in her. There is a poorer chance for a constructive outcome in this situation.

Children must be allowed to express anger, and even rage. They must also be permitted to vent feelings of despair, to seek comfort when they are fearful, and to share experiences of delight and joy as well. Chapter 7 describes some methods you can use to help your children talk through their feelings. However, an important first step in this process is the recognition that emotional expressiveness is a vital key to emotional health.

CAN WE TALK?

It is easier to assess how children are doing emotionally when you actively encourage them to share their feelings. Sometimes they do, and say things that make you want to cringe, and it is tempting to try to squelch talk that makes you feel embarrassed, or frightened. However, if you can hang in there when the going gets scary, and convince them that you truly want to hear whatever they have to say, they'll tell you far more of what's in their hearts. And you'll know far better how much help they actually need.

David was quite disturbed when his six-year-old son, Tim, who was usually a quiet, controlled, and self-contained child, had a violent response to a transgression committed by the family dog. The dog chewed up and nearly destroyed a paperback copy of the adventure story father and son had been reading together at bedtime. When Tim discovered the mangled remains of his treasured book, he seized the dog by the neck, and threatened to torture and kill him. Anxious to quell the boy's rage, David quickly rescued the dog and counseled his son against violent solutions to his problems. He remind Tim that it was his responsibility to care for his possessions, and keep them out of the dog's reach.

As David reflected on his son's outburst later, he felt that he had done the right thing by establishing boundaries for Tim, but he wondered if he should go a bit further. He began to think of his son's extreme reaction to the loss of the book less as an isolated event, and more as a response to the extreme stress the family had been experiencing for months.

David's wife had recently entered a recovery program to deal with a long-standing addiction to alcohol and other psychoactive drugs. Her recovery activities and her work in medical research kept her away from home much of the time. Furthermore, the strain of managing her professional responsibilities while struggling to maintain her sobriety left her feeling anxious, depressed, and fatigued when she was able to be home.

David knew that he often felt emotionally rocky himself—subject to bouts of depression and anger, as well as dread that his wife might start to drink and drug again. He guessed that Tim was grappling with similar feelings, and he knew how hard it was for his son to talk about troubling emotions, or to ask for help with them. Tim's rageful assault on the dog might be his only means of expressing the anguish he felt about the turmoil in the family.

David wanted to make it more possible for his son to speak directly about his reactions to the family trouble, and so he began to make a greater effort to talk to Tim about the problems the family was having and about his own feelings.

At first, David didn't mention his wife's drinking. He told Tim that Mommy was depressed—that sometimes she felt fine and sometimes she was terribly upset. He took care to explain that Mommy's moods were not Tim's problem. He did not cause his mother to be upset, and there was nothing he could do about it when she was feeling bad. David made a practice of repeating this point over and over again to Tim. He also reminded Tim, frequently, that both parents were well aware of the problem Mommy was having, and were working hard to do something about it.

As time went on, David realized that he was presenting an incomplete picture of the family's struggle to Tim, and he began to worry that Tim's attempts to "fill in the blanks" left by the official version of Mommy's illness might leave the child lead to create a far graver, and more frightening vision of the problem than was actually justified. David began to discuss his wife's alcoholism with his son, relating it to habits Tim was struggling with, like biting his nails, so that the child might understand that his mother was trying to do something that was very hard for her to do. David explained that alcohol made Mommy sick, upset, and extremely depressed. He also explained that it was her efforts to conquer her drinking that kept her away from home so much. She needed help to stop drinking, and she had to go outside the home to get this help.

David also began to express his own feelings more openly to Tim. He acknowledged that he sometimes found it hard to manage all of his responsibilities at work and home when Mommy was away, and that even though he knew how hard she was working to get better, he found himself getting frustrated and angry when this happened.

When David and Tim argued, and David felt himself growing angry with his son, he tried hard to speak about his feelings at the moment they were occurring, rather than withdrawing from Tim, or exploding in rage at him. He also shared with Tim that he had felt relieved by his own decision to share some of his troubled feelings with a psychologist, and that it always helped him to talk about his feelings with other people. He assured his son that he would try to be available whenever Tim wanted to talk with him, but he also invited the boy to consider speaking with a therapist of his own.

David returned to such themes time and again in conversations with his son. The two frequently used the bedtime hour as a time to share feelings about good and bad things that had happened during the day. When Tim was able to share some feeling of fear, anger or insecurity, David would try to validate his son's experience by describing his own similar reactions to the same kinds of circumstances.

This strategy eventually paid off for David and Tim. It took time, but the boy became increasingly able to speak directly about important feelings he experienced at home, and at school, and with friends. David also found that Tim was far more likely to look to him for comfort in situations that were troubling to him. After several months of talks and sharing, and a few weeks after his mother had experienced a brief relapse, Tim said to his father, "Dad, I'm having that trouble sleeping again, and I haven't really been feeling too good about myself lately. I think maybe it would be a good idea if I talked to a psychologist."

Psychological and Emotional Health: An Overall View

Psychological and emotional health includes:

- The absence of significant emotional illness
- The ability to make rewarding use of native interests and abilities

- The ability to identify and express important aspects of one's emotional experience to supportive peers and adult guides
- The ability to ask for support, assistance, and advice at appropriate times, from helpful people inside and outside the family
- The capacity to muster and apply internal resources to solve difficult problems

The Inevitability of Stress and Conflict. It is important to understand that children have so many and such complex developmental hurdles to clear, that they cannot avoid setbacks, delays, and psychological conflict on their journey to psychological maturity and health. Children frequently show a somewhat uneven pattern of development, acquiring skills quickly and easily in some areas, while needing additional support and encouragement in some others. Furthermore, no child is able to do well under every condition and circumstance.

Emotional well-being is not defined by the absence of stress and conflict. On the contrary, it depends, in part, on the ability to accept and cope constructively with the pressures and disappointments that are an inevitable element of human life.

Understanding Psychological Disorders

Because some degree of stress and conflict is a normal and necessary part of childhood development (as it is normal and necessary at every stage of human development), it can be hard to determine when a particular problem is sufficiently severe and of sufficient long-standing to be called a "disorder." Physical illness tends to be a simpler call, because everyone knows that fever and vomiting are "abnormal" and that they should arouse concern in a parent. But if children are always handling some degree of pressure and challenge, how is a parent to know when real concern is justified?

Even though the picture is more cloudy and complicated when one is assessing emotional problems, the process of making a decision about the need for professional assistance is roughly similar to the one you use when you decide whether or not your pediatrician should look at that rash or palpate that aching tummy. When your child is physically ill, and you need to decide whether to call the doctor, you observe his symptoms, consider how bad he feels and how long he has felt that way, and whether he is showing signs of improvement. You don't try to diagnose him, and you don't try to treat chronic or severe symptoms. Your focus and your problem-solving efforts are directed at deciding whether to get a professional assessment of the need for treatment. This should also be your focus when emotional problems arise in a child. You must ask yourself, "Do I need help in understanding what is going on here, and in figuring out what to do about it?" In answering this question you must consider the following issues:

- Whether your child is displaying symptoms of emotional illness
- Whether the symptoms present an immediate threat to health and physical well-being
- Whether the symptoms have been evident for several weeks or more
- Whether the symptoms are interfering with his ability to learn, to play, or to establish meaningful relationships with peers and elders
- Whether the symptoms seem to improve with additional family and/or school support

Questions about the duration and severity of a symptom and the degree of impairment a child is experiencing always involve a subjective judgment by a parent. A self-help text can provide information to guide that judgment, but such information will only be helpful if you feel ready to acknowledge the possibility that your child may be in real pain. It is harder to identify emotional disorders in children than it is to recognize their physical maladies, and it is often harder for a parent to accept a child's emotional pain than it is to acknowledge his physical suffering. This is because when a child is hurting emotionally, parents frequently feel to blame for his distress. Shame and guilt can lead you to deny symptoms of emotional disorder in your child, just as they can lead you to disavow problematic drinking in yourself or your partner. As you read the following sections, which discuss symptoms of disorders that are sometimes seen in children of alcoholics, try to keep an open mind and vow that if you err, you will err onthe side of caution. In other words, promise yourself that if this material arouses concern about your child's emotional well-being, you will secure a professional opinion about the need for treatment.

Problems in Infancy and Early Childhood

Failure to Thrive. Sometimes an infant or young child loses a great deal of weight, or fails to gain weight as expected. If a child's weight remains well below the norms for his age and height for an extended period, a physician may diagnose the condition of failure to thrive (FTT).

Some children are small for reasons of heredity, and their size does not affect their overall health. But children who fail to thrive are not getting the nutrients they need to grow normally and maintain good health. Sometimes this disorder has a physical origin, and sometimes it is caused by eating problems that reflect an underlying emotional disorder. In many cases, FTT results from a combination of adverse physical and emotional factors.

FTT that stems from emotional factors usually develops by the age of one, and may appear in infants under six months. Children with this disorder appear to be underweight and may be short of stature as well. Posture may be affected, so that the child either appears to droop or sag or else to stand rigidly erect. Whether FTT is physically or emotionally based, a child with the disorder may vomit or have frequent bouts of diarrhea. His mood may be irritable, and he may be withdrawn, preferring solitary play to any social interaction.

Potential complications of FTT include ongoing problems in maintaining adequate weight, difficulties in school adjustment, learning problems, and the development of certain behavioral disorders. An early diagnosis and timely treatment of FTT is critical to the prevention of these kinds of complications.

Sleep Disorders. Children display a variety of problems with sleep that can be disruptive to the household, but, because they resolve themselves over time, are not a cause for serious concern. During the first year of life, parents are most often upset because their children do not sleep through the night. Two-year-olds may be reluctant to go to sleep, and they may have frequent nightmares. During the years between three and five, children may have trouble falling asleep, and they may experience sleep terrors (experiences of confusion and extreme fright that occur during very deep sleep). Children of this age are also subject to nightmares and nighttime awakenings. Many young children also experience one or two incidents of walking or talking in their sleep. Occasional insomnia is normal in children, as it is among adults, and is usually associated with an identifiable emotional or physical stressor.

Some children in alcoholic families develop chronic sleep disorders because their parents argue violently at nighttime (perhaps when the alcoholic finally returns home after an evening of drinking and carousing), or because they are afraid that an argument or accident will occur as a result of a parent's loss of control. (For example, many children of alcoholics report slipping out of bed after their parents have retired to make sure that cigarettes or stoves have not been left burning.) Most sleep problems that children experience are eventually outgrown, but professional assistance is required if these problems do become chronic and/or begin to interfere with the child's daytime functioning.

Eating Disorders. Three types of eating problems tend to occur during infancy or early childhood, and each can cause serious medical problems. Children who continually eat nonfood items may have *pica*, a disorder usually seen in children under the age of three. Some young children habitually force themselves to regurgitate partially digested food. This disorder is referred to as *rumination.* Other children chronically *overeat,* and become obese. All three of these problems deserve prompt medical attention. Pica and rumination are disorders that can lead to acute medical emergencies.

Hyperactivity and Attention-Deficit Disorder. The hyperactive child, excitable, restless, and perpetually in motion, often shows problems with attention as well. He may have difficulty concentrating and be easily distracted, and his behavior may seem impulsive, as if he has not thought through the consequences of his acts. Children with attention-deficit disorder (ADD) may shift mood quickly and become frustrated easily. Some children with ADD have behavioral problems, such as frequent temper tantrums. These disorders may have a physiological basis, but underlying anxiety and depression can also produce distractibility and an agitated mood.

ADD is most often diagnosed when children enter school and are unable to exert the self-control necessary to perform quiet work at a desk or to complete a relatively complex, but age-appropriate project. However, there may be signs of the disorder even in infancy, as the baby has difficulty developing regular feeding and sleeping patterns, and seems to feel overstimulated and irritated by attempts to touch or cuddle him.

Toddlers with ADD find it hard to focus for any extended period on a single toy, or a television program, or a storybook. They are often extremely hungry for attention, and tend to be intrusive and impulsive. They are curious about everything and insistent on exploring everything. They require fairly constant supervision because they tend to be oblivious to danger.

Hyperactivity and ADD frequently lead to poor school adjustment and real difficulty in peer interactions. These problems, in turn, lead to severe deficits in self-esteem, as well as social alienation. Early diagnosis and treatment can prevent the development of these unfortunate complications.

Autism. Autism is a developmental disorder that has disturbing and far-reaching effects on an affected child's social and intellectual functioning, and on his development and use of language.

Autistic children typically have very great difficulty forming emotional attachments to their parents and to other people. Sometimes, this difficulty with bonding appears even in infancy, with babies displaying indifference to cuddling or holding. An older baby may fail to make eye contact with others, smile infrequently or not at all, and have difficulty recognizing people who should be familiar to him. Autistic children often appear to dwell in a world of their own.

With time, autistic children may become more attached and more responsive to parents. However, they usually continue to struggle greatly with peer relationships, since they have little ability to play cooperatively or to sense and respond to the feelings of others.

Language difficulties are quite pronounced in autistic children. Some exhibit a lifelong inability to speak, whereas others develop a capacity for speech, but habitually echo sounds and words emitted by others, sometimes repeating, word for word, entire conversations they have overheard. When autistic children do develop meaningful speech, they often commit grammatical errors, experience great difficulty remembering the names of objects, and use pronouns incorrectly. It is also hard for them to talk about abstract concepts.

Autistic children may seem over-responsive to some stimuli and under-responsive to others. They often have a compelling need for sameness in their lives, and can become intensely distressed over any effort to change the details of their environment or daily routine. Sometimes the need for sameness and repetition is displayed in habitual and compulsive hair pulling, headbanging, or rocking.

The overall rate of development in autistic children is very uneven. For example, a child may walk at a very early age, but fail to become toilet trained for several years.

Autistic children require constant care as well as highly specialized educational and treatment interventions. In order to learn how to best utilize the skills and understandings they do have, these youngsters need to receive an early diagnosis of their disorder and enroll in an ongoing treatment program as soon as possible.

Fetal Alcohol Syndrome and Fetal Alcohol Effects. When an expectant mother drinks, the alcohol she ingests is quickly distributed to all fetal tissues. The highest concentrations of alcohol appear to occur in the liver, pancreas, kidney, lung, thymus, heart, and brain of the unborn child. Research has not established the level of alcohol consumption during pregnancy which places an unborn child at risk, and it may be impossible to do so. However, since the results of drinking during pregnancy are potentially disastrous for the developing fetus, physicians usually advise expectant mothers to abstain completely during pregnancy.

Fetal alcohol effects (FAE) may be seen in any or all of the child's organ systems, but the effects most likely to be noticed by parents include:

- Reduced birth weight (often associated with premature delivery of the infant)
- Failure to thrive (with resulting postnatal growth retardation)
- Head and facial abnormalities, such as
  - A short, upturned nose, with an underdeveloped bridge
  - Large ears that are low-set and, perhaps, rotated toward the back of the head

- Small and wide-set eyes, with drooping eyelids
- A wide mouth, perhaps with cleft lip or cleft palate, or poorly formed teeth
- Disorders of the central nervous system, including
  - Mental retardation
  - Cerebral palsy
  - Hyperactivity
  - Learning disabilities
  - Seizures
  - Sleep problems

A physician may diagnose fetal alcohol syndrome if she determines that there has been prenatal or postnatal growth retardation, and that facial anomalies and central nervous system dysfunctions characteristic of FAS are also present. If these three criteria are not met, but other symptoms associated with alcohol abuse during pregnancy are present, and the child's mother is known to be alcoholic, the physician may conclude that there are fetal alcohol effects (FAE).

There is no treatment to reverse FAS or FAE, but accurate and early diagnosis is still desirable. If parents and teachers understand the source of behavioral and cognitive deficits in a child, they are in a position to tailor learning and living situations to meet the child's special needs and enable him to reach his full developmental potential.

Problems in Later Childhood and Adolescence

Anxiety Disorders. The experience of fear is quite common in children, with specific kinds of fears tending to appear at particular ages. For example, infants typically display a fear of strangers between the ages of six and nine months, whereas two-year-olds are often haunted by visions of imaginary creatures. Four-year-olds are frequently fearful of the dark, and older children characteristically dread social rejection and academic failure. Periodic, transient episodes of anxiousness or fearfulness in children are usually not a cause for concern. But if there is a prolonged period of uneasiness, or episodes that are so intense as to interfere with the child's subjective sense of well-being and his day-to-day functioning, you should consult a professional helper.

The *overanxious* child may not be able to specify a particular fear, but may seem extremely self-conscious and worried about his competence, or his ability to perform at school or sports. He may have nervous habits, such as nail biting, and there may be some sort of sleep disturbance. Sometimes an overanxious child has a recurring physical symptom, such as a stomachache, or a headache. He tends to worry about the future a great deal, and may require frequent calming and reassurance.

Some children have highly focused fears, called *phobias.* Phobic children are so frightened that they absolutely avoid the situation or object that arouses terror. Just the thought of the dreaded object may stir feelings of fear and panic, and the child may even express a fear that he will die if he is forced to confront the problematic situation.

Children can become fearful of many different objects and situations. Some common phobias involve the fear of failure in social or academic situations, being injured in an accident or natural disaster, being hurt by a particular animal, or having to go to a doctor or a hospital. Adults with phobias usually sense that their fear is irrational and inappropriate. Children are not always able to make the distinction between reasonable and unreasonable fears.

The experience of panic is highly unpleasant, and phobic children, who have had a few encounters with it, may begin to fear the panic as much as they fear the panic-inducing object. When this happens, they may severely restrict their activities in an effort to ensure that a panic reaction will not be triggered. For instance, a child who is afraid of dogs may begin by avoiding certain houses and streets where he knows he is likely to encounter a dog. Later on, he may refuse to go outside and play at all, because he knows that once he goes out he will start to worry about the possibility of a dog wandering into his yard, and he does not want to take the chance that this worry will trigger a full-blown panic attack. Early intervention can prevent a phobic reaction from expanding in this way and becoming terribly disabling to the child. When panic symptoms are very severe, medication may be used, along with psychological interventions, to moderate them.

Some children develop a phobia about going to school. They experience extreme anxiety and disturbing physical symptoms (such as dizziness, nausea, stomachache, and headache) that may frighten parents into allowing them to remain at home. The term *school refusal* is often used to describe a situation in which a child is frequently absent from school for extended periods. School refusal is a serious problem, and, once again, parents should seek evaluation and intervention at an early point, before the child's anxiety becomes entrenched and more difficult to treat.

Obsessions and Compulsions. Children may be troubled by the constant intrusion of disturbing thoughts called *obsessions,* or they feel compelled to repeat certain stereotyped behaviors, called *compulsions.* Some children struggle with both obsessions and compulsions. Some obsessions that commonly trouble children involve the possibility of being contaminated by contact with dirt or germs; the dread of illness or injury to the self or beloved others; and the need for extreme orderliness, neatness, or exactness. Common compulsions include excessive handwashing, bathing, or toothbrushing, the repetition of certain rituals, such as going in or out of a door, and a need to check and recheck doors, locks, appliances, or homework. When recurring thoughts and compulsive acts dominate a child's life and interfere with his normal functioning, parents should seek professional help.

Childhood Depression and Suicide. Depressed children are unhappy for extended periods of time. They seem unable to feel pleasure during these periods, and may withdraw from social relationships and other activities that were formerly satisfying to them. Depressed children often do poorly in school because they are unable to concentrate. Their self-esteem is low, and they tend to have a variety of physical complaints. Parents may note a change in sleeping patterns as a child sleeps more or less than usual. Eating habits may also change so that the child eats far less than usual or far more than usual. Some children will brood when depressed, whereas others will try to fight their sadness with bursts of frenetic activity.

Depression can be a prelude to *suicidal behavior.* Therefore, parents should intervene early when a child seems depressed, and seek professional guidance. Immediate action should be taken if a child stops planning for the future, begins to give away treasured possessions, speaks of the possibility of suicide, or the hopelessness or meaninglessness of life, or writes notes or letters that contain these kind of anguished thoughts. When a child speaks of the possibility of suicide, or makes a suicidal gesture, he must always be taken seriously. Even when suicide is an impulsive act, there is almost always some indication that a child is troubled. Professionals find that about three-quarters of all people who commit suicide have given some warning of their intent to kill themselves. The horror that parents feel about the possibility of a child's death often leads them to ignore or discount threats of suicide. Children do become severely depressed, and suicide is the third leading cause of death among adolescents. This is an issue that must be faced squarely by adults. Children who speak of suicide, make suicidal gestures, or exhibit other of the symptoms previously described should be carefully evaluated by a mental health professional who is experienced in working with children.

Eating Disorders. Anorexia nervosa is an eating disorder that typically appears in adolescence and involves a persistent refusal to eat. Anorectic children are usually well underweight. Some anorectic children lose weight by dieting and exercising compulsively.

Anorectic children refuse to gain weight, and they experience (and usually express) an intense fear of getting fat. Most feel fat, even when they appear emaciated to other people. During the early stages of the disorder, parents may notice a startling change in the child's approach to food and eating. For example, some anorectic children cut food into very small pieces or crumble it, and some refuse to eat with the family. Many will eat only one or two foods. Although anorectic children will not eat, they are obsessed by the idea of food and may occupy themselves with preparing food for other people.

Once there is a marked weight loss, and parents begin to express concern, an affected child will often take measures to conceal the disorder by dressing in bulky clothing or by drinking large quantities of water before being weighed. As body weight continues to drop, anorectic children experience weakness, fatigue, lightheadedness, and constipation. Blood pressure drops, and heart rate slows. Amenorrhea (the absence of menstrual periods) is common in adolescent girls with this disorder.

The medical complications of anorexia nervosa can be severe. Congestive heart failure may occur if the anorectic patient suddenly drinks large amounts of water. Furthermore, persistent vomiting critically lowers the concentration of potassium in the bloodstream. Severe potassium deficiency can cause cardiac arrhythmias and sudden death.

Bulimia nervosa is another eating disorder that tends to develop during adolescence. It involves repeated episodes of binge eating and the use of laxatives, diuretics, self-induced vomiting, dieting, or rigorous exercise to avoid weight gain. Bulimic patients feel unable to control their eating during a binge and may keep eating until abdominal pain becomes so severe that they are unable to continue. They are extremely preoccupied with the shape of their body and their weight, although they tend to be of normal size or slightly overweight.

The bulimic patient's persistent vomiting can cause erosion of tooth enamel, swelling of the salivary glands, and irritation of the throat and esophagus. Dehydration may also occur, and the child may suffer from vitamin and mineral deficiencies. Menstrual cycles in bulimic girls may become irregular or they may cease.

The chronic abuse of laxatives can produce rectal bleeding and the loss of potassium. Again, low potassium levels can lead to cardiac arrhythmias and death.

Like chemically dependent patients, individuals with eating disorders often resist treatment, and insist that nothing is wrong with them. Early intervention is critical, however, to disrupt the development of an entrenched obsession with food and to avoid the severe health complications associated with both anorexia and bulimia.

Other Addictive Behaviors. Children who grow up in alcoholic, codependent families often develop addictions of their own. Some experts believe that a predisposition to addictive behaviors can be inherited. It is probably true that social learning, and the need to obliterate the pain associated with life in a troubled family, also fuel addictive behavior.

The word addiction causes thoughts of alcohol and other drugs to spring instantly to mind. However, parents should understand that any substance, or any activity, that alters a child's unpleasant mood and reduces his psychological or physical pain, can become addicting. The eating problems described in this chapter are essentially addictive problems, and exercise, gambling, and spending frequently become problematic for children who grow up in alcoholic homes. Parents are pleased when their children work hard to excel in school, or in extracurricular activities, or at part-time jobs. But a child's involvement in academics, hobbies, or work can also become all-consuming, and therefore destructive to his overall development. People can also become compulsive about sexual activity, and about relationships.

The easiest way to understand addiction is to consider how it contrasts with normal, healthy functioning. Once again, psychological health involves the ability to form meaningful relationships, to express native interests and talents in creative work, and to articulate significant aspects of one's internal, emotional existence to significant and supportive others. Addicted individuals are so deeply involved with a particular drug or a particular activity that it is impossible for life to be maintained in this kind of balanced way. Addiction progresses in stages, but eventually so much psychic energy is devoted to pursuing and engaging the addictive object, that there is nothing left for anything or anyone else. For example, the workaholic finds a brief respite from inner pain in the triumphs of her professional life. However, she becomes so dedicated to the acquisition of status, power, and money that she ignores her deeper need for emotional intimacy, and neglects her family's emotional needs as well. The compulsive spender is often haunted by feelings of internal emptiness, which she hopes to evade by accumulating material goods. The experience of shopping and spending absorbs her and alters her psychological and emotional state so profoundly that she is only transiently aware of her internal discontent. Her emotional detachment damages her capacity for creative self-expression and emotional intimacy (which represent the only real solution to feelings of loneliness and emotional isolation). The chemically dependent person destroys self-awareness, creativity, and the possibility of real emotional intimacy with drugs that deeply distort her self-experience.

There are many approaches to determining whether or not an individual is addicted to a chemical or to an activity. The most precise and most elegant definition of dependency I have ever found is offered by Vernon Johnson, in his book, *I'll Quit Tomorrow* (see the Suggested Reading section). Johnson, in his discussion of alcoholism, argues that a harmful dependency on alcohol exists when usage begins to cause real trouble in some area of an individual's life and she continues to drink. Johnson points out that normal drinkers stop or drastically alter their drinking pattern when their behavior under the influence gets them into some difficulty at work, at home, or in the community at large. Harmfully dependent drinkers may vow to change, and may actually stop drinking, or cut back for a time. Eventually, however, they revert to the old, problematic pattern of usage, and begin to get into trouble again.

You can use Johnson's definition of "harmful dependence" to distinguish healthy involvements with substances, activities, and people, from compulsive ones. When you apply his standard, you will not emphasize the amount of involvement a child has with a certain object or situation. Rather, you will pay close attention to the pattern of his involvement and the manner in which he is, or is not, able to alter this pattern if his behavior begins to cause trouble in his life.

If a child is compulsively involved with food or with psychoactive chemicals, he will probably try to conceal this fact from you. You will see that he is getting into trouble, but you will have to speculate about the root cause of his difficulties. The classic behavioral signs of a growing dependence on alcohol or other drugs include:

- Involvement with peers who are inclined to use drugs
- Loss of interest in activities (e.g., sports or hobbies) that were formerly valued
- Decline of interest and performance at school
- Development of legal problems, including arrests for shoplifting and housebreaking and citations for driving under the influence
- Theft of money or other valuables from parents
- Possession of paraphernalia associated with drug use
- Frequent episodes of obvious intoxication

Parents should also be alert for signs of an acute, toxic reaction to a psychoactive substance. Unexplained, dramatic changes in mental alertness require immediate medical attention. Extreme drowsiness and sluggishness, insomnia, confusion, dizziness, seizure, hallucinations, and loss of consciousness can be signs of a toxic reaction to alcohol or some other drug.

Other common signs of toxicity are dilated or constricted pupils, nausea, vomiting, difficulty with coordination, heavy sweating, chills, shaking, and headache. A child with any of these symptoms may also display a dramatic mood change. He may be panicky, rageful, euphoric, or depressed for no apparent reason.

A final note: Because alcohol is a legal and socially sanctioned drug, parents may become complacent about a child's drinking even when he is underage. However, among the common drugs of abuse, alcohol is the most toxic to human cells and has the capacity to inflict severe damage on every organ system in the human body. Furthermore, it has such profound and adverse effects on judgment, coordination, and emotional control that the drinker, especially the inexperienced drinker, is at grave risk for accidental injury or death. In fact, accidents are the leading cause of death among adolescents, and most of these accidents are alcohol-related.

Conduct Disorders. Children who are so aggressive, oppositional, and destructive that they chronically violate the rights of others, as well as important, age-appropriate behavioral norms, should receive professional attention. Some children commit antisocial acts on their own initiative, and others become involved in delinquent behavior as a result of their involvement with a group or gang of delinquent friends. The following sorts of behaviors are associated with chronic conduct problems:

- Stealing
- Running away from home
- Lying
- Setting fires
- Truancy from school or work
- House- or car-breaking
- Deliberately destroying others' property
- Being physically cruel to animals
- Being physically cruel to people
- Exhibiting sexual aggressiveness or assaultiveness
- Using weapons in fights
- Initiating physical fights

If your child exhibits one or more of these behaviors, and the problem persists for a period of several weeks, you should seek professional help.

Reactions to Traumatic Stress. Children who observe or experience episodes of violence or sexual and physical abuse at home typically experience a great many problems, so that their functioning in a variety of areas is compromised.

Abused children frequently display odd changes in eating behavior, and may binge, purge, and/or hoard food. Bed-wetting and encopresis are frequently associated with the stress of physical or sexual abuse, and abused children may also become constipated as a result of avoiding elimination. Some abused children develop odd rituals around elimination. Some children who had previously achieved toilet training lose this skill as a result of abuse.

An abused child is typically very anxious and may be particularly fearful at bedtime. He may have great difficulty falling asleep as memories of traumatic incidents frequently emerge in the twilight period just before sleep. Furthermore, abused children often have vivid and terrifying nightmares; some walk and talk in their sleep.

Development of age-appropriate skills and academic gains are often delayed in abused children. They may appear withdrawn and unresponsive in school, and have difficulty concentrating and paying attention. In some cases, an abused child may achieve normally for awhile, then show a sharp decrement in performance for an extended period. Then, performance may pick up, only to decline again at a later time.

Sexually abused children often display inappropriate and aggressive sexual behavior in play or at school. They may expose themselves, use provocative language, touch others in a sexual way, or exhibit unusually advanced knowledge of sex. These children may not remember committing sexually inappropriate acts.

Abused children may be unusually aggressive or unusually passive in their behavior toward others. Some alternate between a pattern of aggression and a more passive, depressed, withdrawn, and dependent posture with peers and elders. At times, they may seem to provoke other children or adults into behaving abusively toward them.

Sexually and physically abused children may have physical symptoms as well. Headaches are common, as are tics. Some children may experience numbness in a part of the body or express a conviction that some part of the body, which appears intact, has actually been damaged.

Symptoms such as these deserve immediate attention from a professional who is familiar with the problem of traumatic stress and physical and sexual abuse. A quick, effective response to stress reactions is necessary to prevent the development of severe and chronic emotional disorder and to interrupt the cycle of abuse at home.

Childhood Psychosis. A very few children develop a severe disturbance of language, thought, and learning called *schizophrenia*. The earliest sign of childhood schizophrenia may be language problems that reflect the child's disorganized thought processes. The child may have trouble placing words in an appropriate context, and may have difficulty understanding that some words can have several different meanings. He may string words together that have little or no relation to one another, in a sort of "word salad," for example, "I have a car, bar, star, jar like a can, man, fan." Schizophrenic children often make up words, and may frequently echo words and sentences uttered by others. For all these reasons, the speech of a schizophrenic child tends to be bizarre and often incomprehensible to others.

Schizophrenic children have trouble learning from experience, and may be repeatedly injured because they fail to comprehend that certain situations or objects are dangerous. Nonetheless, they are subject to a variety of irrational fears and phobias.

Children with schizophrenia tend to have many social difficulties. They may be socially withdrawn, tending to concentrate on one toy or one solitary activity for hours on end. They often seem socially inept, with a marked inability to appreciate social boundaries. They may frequently interrupt others or habitually stand too close or too far away when conversing with others. It may be hard for them to understand that others do not think or feel the same things that they think and feel. Their mood may often seem flat or they may laugh, cry, or erupt in anger at inappropriate times.

Some schizophrenic children show motor deficiencies, such as physical awkwardness, poor coordination, and peculiar posture.

As schizophrenic children reach school age, they may begin to have *hallucinations* and *delusions*. Delusions usually take the form of a highly inflated, grandiose self-image, and irrational suspicions about the intent and motives of other people. Children who hallucinate usually see people or animals or things that are not present or hear sounds or voices that are not present.

Childhood schizophrenia may develop gradually or suddenly, and it may become chronic, although this does not always happen. Schizophrenic children require specialized educational and treatment programs to help them to learn and overcome their most serious disabilities. Medication may also be useful in helping some schizophrenic children to function better.

Parents of schizophrenic children benefit greatly from supportive counseling and the guidance and encouragement that can be obtained from other parents of schizophrenic children.

Conclusion

Many of the symptoms and disorders described in this chapter are believed to have a genetic component. In other words, children may have an inherited vulnerability to certain psychological and emotional problems. These problems are more likely to flare when a predisposed child is exposed to chronic, intense stress and does not have access to adult support and guidance as he struggles to manage this stress.

As a therapeutic parent, you will need to make a critical judgment when signs of distress appear in your child. Does this change in behavior, performance, or mood represent a passing storm, or might it signal the onset of a significant problem that requires professional assessment and intervention? Use the information presented here, and in the Suggested

Reading section that describe normal patterns of development in child-hood, and consider the following questions:

- How long have these problems existed?
- How many areas of my child's functioning have been affected, and how severely? For example:
  - Has school performance declined?
  - Is his behavior or mood making it difficult for him to get along with family members?
  - Is his behavior or mood alienating his friends, or attracting the wrong sort of companions?
  - Is he losing his capacity to enjoy activities that gave him pleasure in the past?
  - Is he losing his confidence in himself and his faith in other people?
  - *Is his behavior threatening his physical health or survival?*

It is also important to listen to what your child says about his emotional state. Children in pain often try to signal their distress, although they often do this in an indirect way. For example, it is quite unusual for a child to approach a parent and say, as the boy described at the outset of this chapter said to his father, "I'm not feeling so good about myself, and I think I should see a psychologist." However, children who are losing confidence in themselves may well say, with some frequency and some intensity, "I always make mistakes. I can't get anything right. I'm just stupid." Use the active listening skills presented in chapter 7 to help your child talk more fully and more deeply about such feelings. If you think he is feeling miserable, tell him so and tell him that it is okay for him to talk to you about it. Make it okay for him to talk by using reflection and restatement and by holding back anxious remarks that may sound critical and disapproving to him.

You can often get valuable information about your child and his struggles from his teachers. Regard their comments about disturbing changes in your child's behavior or mood seriously, and ask for a conference where you can get specific information about incidents that have aroused the school's concern.

Finally, take an active, deliberate approach to your child's emotional distress. Trust your intuition when it tells you your child is hurting and hurting badly. And, as you consider whether or not to secure professional help, take a cue from the old sailing maxim about shortening sails when the wind begins to build:

- If you think about it, DO IT.

= 10 =

Finding Good Professional Help

Finding good professional help is not an easy process for most people. My own experience, though, was an exception to this rule. I began to consider psychotherapy during my twenties, when I was a graduate student. A friend of mine, who had recently graduated from the academic program I was attending and who was struggling with problems that were similar to my own, was already seeing a psychologist she liked a great deal. When she discovered that her therapist had an hour open on Thursday mornings, she called me to see if I happened to be free at the same time. In fact, I did not have any classes or clinical appointments at that hour, and so, on my friend's advice, I called her therapist and scheduled a consultation. I found myself in treatment before I had consciously decided that this was what I wanted to do. Fortunately, the therapist my friend chose for me was a good match. It took a while, but eventually my whole life changed for the better.

In retrospect, I'm amazed that I acted as impulsively and blindly as I did, and still managed to get the help I needed. As a graduate student in a mental health field, I knew very well that therapists, even therapists with the same professional identity and specialty, differ widely in their training, their experience, and their personality type. My confusion and embarrassment about needing therapy led me to take the path of least resistance (and least reflection) to treatment. I had a recommendation from a friend, and my schedule coincided with that of the psychologist she recommended. A lot of people with less knowledge of the mental health professions than I had in graduate school make decisions about psychological treatment in this same way. Some are lucky, as I was. However, many find that what worked well for a friend will not work for them at all. This happens quite often to people who need help for prob-

149

lems related to alcoholism and codependency, and who obtain referrals from friends whose conflicts have a different origin.

Alcoholics and their families need specialized services. However, feelings of shame and pessimism about the prospects for lasting change can present an enormous impediment to finding and using these services. Such feelings prevent families in need from entering treatment during the early stages of the disease, when it is most treatable. They also cause people to act impulsively, and sometimes unwisely, when they do seek professional help.

If you have decided to consult a mental health professional on your own behalf, or for your children, then your courage has triumphed over the humiliation and hopelessness that might have pulled you and your family more deeply into the disease of alcoholism. You've taken an extremely important step, but you still face some further challenging decisions. You have to choose a therapist who is right for you and your family—one who is well-trained, ethical, experienced in the treatment of addictions, and whose personality and personal style are suited to your own.

The number and type of practitioners who offer psychological services today are quite vast. The field includes psychiatrists; clinical, counseling, and school psychologists; clinical social workers; mental health counselors; and others. The task of choosing from among this array can feel daunting, especially when you are under a great deal of emotional pressure, and if you have had no significant previous experience with mental health services. This chapter organizes and simplifies this task to some degree by providing basic information about academic and professional credentials that mental health professionals should possess if they offer clinical services. The type of training and experience they should have if they provide treatment to chemically dependent families is described, and some questions are listed that you can pose to a prospective therapist to determine whether she has specialized knowledge in the field of addictions. Finally, the chapter describes the personal characteristics of mental health practitioners that are often important in determining whether clients feel comfortable with their choice of a therapist, and satisfied that they have found a "good fit."

Beginning the Search

Most people are searching for answers when they make the decision to enter psychotherapy. The last thing they want to confront is a series of confusing questions about how and where to get help. But the array of helpers and services available is so broad that it can't help but raise a number of important questions. For instance, what is the difference between a psychologist, a psychiatrist, and a clinical social worker? Who is most likely to have experience with addicted people and their families? If you, your spouse, and your children all seem to need professional assistance, can you all get it in the same place?

The most obvious sort of distinction that can be made among mental health professionals involves their academic training and the particular credentials that each possesses. This, however, is only one of many distinctions that can be made among practitioners. Most consumers begin with this information because it is easily accessible. Furthermore, any reasonable person would want to be sure that a prospective therapist had received adequate training in the provision of psychological services and had mastered fundamental concepts in human development and psychopathology.

However, professional credentials do not, in and of themselves, guarantee the type and quality of treatment that will be provided. Furthermore, the degree and license obtained by a specific practitioner provide absolutely no information about his or her qualifications to provide treatment to a family with problems involving alcohol, drugs, and codependency. So it is important to regard the following information, which reviews the type of training, and the type of certification, received by different kinds of mental health practitioners, as a jumping-off point in your search for a therapist.

What's in a Name?

Most states reserve certain professional designations, including *psychiatrist, psychologist* and *licensed clinical social worker,* for individuals who have completed a prescribed course of academic training and who have completed the examinations necessary to obtain professional credentials in their field of specialization. Therefore, it is usually safe to assume that practitioners who use one of these titles have met certain basic academic and professional standards.

Psychiatrists are medical doctors who have completed four years of college, four years of medical school, a year-long clinical internship, and a residency (or course of specialized training) in psychiatry that lasts four years. Psychiatrists must complete an additional two years of training if they wish to be qualified in a subspeciality of psychiatry. For example, a *child psychiatrist* must complete a two-year fellowship in this specialty area in order to represent herself as a child psychiatrist.

After the psychiatrist completes her academic and clinical training and chooses the state in which she plans to practice, she must meet the qualifications for licensure as a physician in that state. These qualifications typically include completing written and oral examinations that assess whether basic concepts in medicine have actually been mastered during the course of training the individual has completed.

Some psychiatrists also choose to obtain "Board Certification" in general psychiatry. Psychiatric boards are more rigorous examinations than those required for licensure. Licensing exams assess one's com-petency to practice medicine. General psychiatry boards test candidates on the more specialized body of information that makes up psychiatry. Some psychiatrists elect to become board certified in subspecialities, such as child psychiatry. This requires them to take additional examinations. Psychiatrists who are board certified generally display certificates attesting to this fact in their offices. If you do not see such a certificate, and wish to know whether your psychiatrist is board certified, you should feel free to ask her.

Since medical knowledge is always changing and always expanding, psychiatrists must receive a certain amount of continuing education during their careers if they wish to maintain their license to practice. The amount and type of continuing education that is required are fixed by individual state authorities.

Psychiatrists are trained as physicians and can legally prescribe psychoactive medications that may be helpful in the treatment of some conditions, including some cases of depression and anxiety. Health insurance companies will usually reimburse you for a portion of the fees paid to a psychiatrist.

Psychologists are also called doctor, because they have received advanced degrees called "doctorates" in psychology or in a related field such as education or human development. The doctoral degree may be a Ph.D. (Doctor of Philosophy), Psy.D. (Doctor of Psychology), or Ed.D. (Doctor of Education). In any case, the individual will typically have completed about five years of academic training beyond college and met the requirements for licensure in the state in which she maintains a practice. Requirements for licensure vary from state to state, but usually include a year long clinical internship, a year of supervised, postdoctoral clinical practice, and the successful completion of oral and written examinations that cover basic topics in psychology, mental health and professional ethics and conduct.

Some psychologists also obtain a "diplomate" in their area of specialization, which is akin to board certification for physicians and also involves the completion of additional examinations. In most states, psychologists must receive continuing education in order to maintain their licenses.

Psychologists may not prescribe medicine, but those in independent practice usually have close working relationships with a number of psychiatrists who provide and monitor medication for their patients when it is necessary. Health insurance companies will usually cover a portion of your expenses when you are treated by a licensed psychologist.

Psychology associates are individuals who work under the supervision of a licensed psychologist. They are usually working to meet the requirements for licensure, and while their credentials are still incomplete, the psychologist who supervises their clinical work takes complete responsibility for it. A psychology associate may or may not have a doctoral degree. Some insurance companies provide reimbursement for services provided by a psychology associate.

Licensed clinical social workers usually complete two years of academic study beyond college and receive a master's degree in clinical social work. The academic course provides supervised experience in the provision of psychotherapy and the graduate must obtain further supervised experience in order to qualify for the licensing examination in clinical social work. The examination covers topics in social work and mental health.

Some social workers obtain doctoral degrees in their field. This degree is designated by the initials D.S.W. and indicates that the practitioner has completed additional years of training and research beyond the master's degree. The doctoral degree in social work is an academic, rather than a medical degree. Like psychologists, clinical social workers consult with psychiatrists when their patients require medication. Your insurance company may cover services provided by a clinical social worker, but may require that a physician refer you for these services.

You may consult other professionals who use titles that are not legally defined or protected.

Psychoanalysts are typically psychiatrists who have completed a course of study at a psychoanalytic institute that is approved by the American Psychoanalytic Association. These institutes provide intensive exposure to the ideas and methods of Sigmund Freud and the important analytic thinkers who followed him. Depending on the particular institute they attend, students may also be required to study the work of those contemporary analysts who have sought to alter the concepts and methods of standard psychoanalytic practice. Trainees at approved analytic institutes must undergo a "training analysis" of their own—that is, they must be analyzed by a senior analyst at the institute—in order to receive certification as analysts. They must also present their own clinical work to faculty supervisors, who make the final decisions about whether or not to certify an individual as a psychoanalyst. Psychoanalysts who are psychiatrists and who have obtained state licensure as a physician may prescribe psychoactive medications for their patients.

Psychoanalysts may come from other professional backgrounds as well. For example, a recent court decision required the American Psycho-analytic Association to allow psychologists to train as psychoanalysts. Other practitioners, who are non-physicians, are referred to as lay analysts. These providers have received training at psychoanalytic institutes, but are not permitted to call themselves psychoanalysts by the American Psychoanalytic Association because they are not medical doctors. In general, you should be aware that it is the American Psychoanalytic Association that sets the standards for training of psychoanalysts, not the law. Therefore, you must ask specific questions in order to ascertain the actual training and experience of a clinician who refers to herself as a psychoanalyst.

The terms counselor and psychotherapist also have no legal protection or definition. Anyone can use these titles, and some people do so with only the most minimal kind of academic or professional background in mental health. In other cases, these titles are used by people who have a master's degree in a mental health field and fairly extensive experience and supervision in clinical practice. You will have to ask specific questions about an individual's training in order to determine whether a person who calls himself a psychotherapist or a counselor has a university degree in mental health and has had adequate professional experience to treat you and your family. See the section in this chapter entitled *The Consultation*, below, for some questions that may be helpful.

The Addictions Specialist

Just as different people can become depressed for different reasons, different people become addicted to the same chemicals for very different reasons. However, a business executive who becomes depressed when she loses her job will usually have symptoms, such as lethargy, sadness, and changes in eating and sleeping patterns, that are fairly similar to the symptoms that would develop in a neighbor if she became depressed after separating from her husband. A well-trained and relatively experienced mental health professional would make the diagnosis of clinical depression fairly easily in either case, once the prospective patient made an appointment, arrived for a consultation, and described her troubling experiences.

The diagnosis of alcoholism is often a far more complicated matter. First of all, most alcoholics do not voluntarily present themselves for evaluation and treatment of their compulsive drinking. If they do seek treatment on their own initiative, it is likely to be for a physical or behavioral symptom that is secondary to the drinking, such as gastrointestinal distress or performance problems at work or at school. The particular symptom that drives an alcoholic to treatment is usually determined by her specific organic vulnerabilities to alcohol or by the willingness of her partner or her employer to tolerate particular sorts of aberrant behavior. Alcoholics often fail to sense the connection between their symptoms and their drinking, and many do not express concern about their intake of alcohol when they meet with a mental health practitioner. When they don't (and sometimes, even when they do), they are misdiagnosed and mistreated. This is because many professional helpers are unaware of the role alcohol can play in a variety of physical and emotional illnesses and have not been trained to ask leading questions about it.

Codependence is also difficult to diagnose, and for the same reasons. Different individuals are troubled by different symptoms. Patients' presenting complaints are most often determined not by the mere fact of a family member's drinking, but by the pattern of it, and by their own susceptibility to different emotional problems. Some spouses and children of alcoholics become depressed. Others experience periodic episodes of panic, or difficulty concentrating and performing on the job or at school. Still others develop a variety of psychosomatic symptoms, such as headaches, or ulcers. Codependent people, like alcoholics, do not always link physical and emotional distress to drinking by a partner, or by a parent. Even if they do understand that there is a connection, they may feel too frightened or ashamed to report the alcoholic problem to a physician or counselor. If the helping professional has not been taught to ask directly about the role alcohol plays in her patient's life, the serious problem that lies beneath the presenting complaint will not be detected, and an inappropriate course of treatment will be instituted.

For these reasons, recovering alcoholics and recovering family members should seek help from physicians and mental health professionals who have specialized training and experience in the treatment of alcoholism and other compulsive problems. However, an addictions specialist should also be qualified through training and experience to treat the kinds of emotional problems that frequently appear in conjunction with chemical dependency and codependence. For example, depression and anxiety are commonly seen in addicted persons and their spouses and children. These problems seldom disappear as soon as the alcoholic's sobriety is firmly established. In fact, depression and anxiety frequently escalate in the aftermath of sobriety as the alcoholic begins to face her problems without chemical anesthesia, and the family struggles to establish new ways of relating that are not based on the need to conceal, or compensate for, compulsive drinking.

Some psychiatrists, some psychologists, some social workers, and some mental health counselors are trained to do addictions work; others are not. Graduate programs and medical schools are only just beginning to acknowledge that addictions work requires some particular skills and understandings that are not provided in the course of a general education in mental health work. Therefore, practitioners who do have specialized training and experience are likely to have acquired it after they completed their graduate training. Unfortunately, there is no legally protected title, such as addictions specialist, to help you locate a therapist who has both a strong foundation in mental health work and solid preparation in addictions counseling. Some states do have designations, such as *Certified Addictions Counselor,* which guarantee that the individual has completed certain courses in the theory and treatment of chemical dependency. However, this kind of credential usually does not ensure that the certified individual has any other training or experience in the provision of mental health services.

Colleagues in Alcoholics Anonymous, referral boards that are maintained by state psychological and psychiatric associations, and local hospitals that provide treatment for chemical dependency are all potential sources of information about mental health providers who are skilled in addictions work. Regardless of how you obtain a referral, however, there are particular questions you will have to ask a prospective therapist in order to be sure that she, has the specialized training and experience you and your family need. These questions can be posed during, or soon after, your first consultation with a prospective psychotherapist.

The Consultation

Therapists refer to their initial meeting with a new patient as a *consultation*. They approach a consultation a bit differently than they do a regular psychotherapy hour. During the consultation, it is necessary to gather a certain amount of history and other personal data from the patient so that it will be possible to form an impression of her needs, and the therapist will be able to determine whether she feels qualified and willing to provide treatment.

The consultation presents an opportunity for the patient to form impressions as well. During this time, you should begin to ask yourself whether this therapist seems experienced and knowledgeable about chemical dependence and codependence. You should also consider whether you feel welcomed, understood, and respected by this individual. Does it seem possible that you could forge a bond of trust with this person? Can you imagine that, with her, you would eventually feel able to discuss fully the secrets that have been troubling you?

Your impressions will not, and should not, be fully formed by the end of the first hour. However, they should be favorable enough before you make the decision to commit to an extended piece of work with someone. Some therapists do not charge a fee for the initial consultation, because they want patients to feel able to interview two or three therapists before making a firm decision. It is a good idea to have more than one consultation, especially if you feel serious reservations after meeting with the first therapist on your list.

You have a story to tell during the consultation and many questions to ask. You'll probably start with your story, but early on in your relationship with a prospective therapist you must determine if she has specialized knowledge and experience in addictions work. Here are the questions I would ask, and the kinds of answers that I would hope to hear if I were seeking treatment for addiction or codependence:

Q: Do you specialize in treating alcoholism, other chemical addictions, and codependence?

A: The therapist should answer in the affirmative or indicate that she has a general practice, but treats many chemically dependent people and their families. It would *not* reassure me to hear that because a therapist is a psychiatrist, psychologist, social worker, or mental health counselor, she feels qualified to treat any kind of mental health problem.

Q: How long have you been treating these kinds of problems?

A: I think that a minimum of two years in addictions work is essential. However, it would also be acceptable to me if a therapist said that she was just beginning to work with addiction issues, but was practicing under the close supervision of another individual with extensive experience in the field. (Of course, you should also inquire as to the supervisor's credentials.)

Q: What type of training have you had to qualify you for work in the addictions field?

A: There are many possible answers to this question, but look for intensive exposure to the problems of chemically dependent individuals and their families. The addictions specialist should have taken academic coursework in chemical and codependence that was provided by an accredited university, or, she should have completed a training program that was approved by a state drug abuse authority or a relevant professional organization. (State psychological and medical associations generally determine whether privately sponsored training programs meet acceptable professional standards.) The specialist should also have "hands-on experience" with addicts and their families. Look for:

- Two years or more of work in a hospital or clinic that specializes in treating chemical addictions and codependence, or
- Supervised experience in an outpatient private practice that specializes in addictions work.

Q: Do you view alcoholism (or other chemical addiction) as a disease?

A: I would be most comfortable with a therapist who answered this question with a qualified, "yes." Certainly, a professional helper should understand that alcoholism must be treated and sobriety stabilized before other emotional problems can be addressed. And she should be aware that many alcoholics may have a genetic predisposition to alcoholism and that chronic heavy drinking always changes the drinker physiologically. However, some adherents of the "disease model" of alcoholism seem to feel that all the problems of alcoholics and their families will eventually resolve once sobriety is established and a new philosophy of life, based on adherence to the Twelve-Step philosophy, is instituted. Sometimes this happens, but there are other cases in which the alcoholic and members of the alcoholic's family suffer from emotional illnesses that do not automatically remit once sobriety has been established. And they can't establish a new, healthier basis for existence until they are able to work through the lingering effects of childhood abuse or overcome disabling symptoms of depression or panic. Your prospective therapist should be open to the idea that you, or your spouse, or your children, may have more than one problem.

Q: How do you feel about Alcoholics Anonymous, Al-Anon, and other kinds of support groups for alcoholics and their families?

A: Most addictions specialists will have literature and schedules for Twelve-Step programs in their waiting areas or office files. These groups are absolutely essential to the recovery of many alcoholic and codependent persons. It is a serious professional lapse for someone to attempt to treat familial alcoholism without a working knowledge of the Twelve-Step philosophy. On the other hand, the Anonymous groups are not the final answer for every addict, or every codependent family member. A strong network of social and emotional support is crucial during recovery, so your therapist should conduct, or know about, private recovery groups that you can utilize during treatment if Twelve-Step groups don't seem to help you.

Q: Should every member of my family receive some kind of treatment?

A: The needs of each member should be carefully considered, and it should be assumed that everybody in the family has some level of need for information or care around the issue of alcoholism. Addictions specialists understand that everyone in the family is affected by the alcoholism of a parent, and should ask about the condition and behavior of each adult and child in the family. She should know of resources that each member can utilize in recovery, including support groups and professional helpers who are knowledgeable about familial alcoholism and who specialize in treating children. She should also be able to recommend physicians who provide medical treatment and medication to recovering individuals.

Q: What is your philosophy about providing psychoactive medication to recovering alcoholics and recovering family members?

A: I think that psychiatrists, and other mental health professionals who send patients to psychiatrists to be evaluated for medication, should take a very cautious approach to this issue. Alcoholism is, by nature, a relapsing disease, and the use of psychoactive medications seems to increase many alcoholics' vulnerability to relapse. Furthermore, many alcoholics are already, or can easily become, cross-addicted to drugs that have the same mechanism of action. This is a particular problem with certain antianxiety agents such as Valium and Librium. Furthermore, highly stressed family members are often prone to develop addictions of their own. On the other hand, there are times when psychoactive medications can be an enormous boon to recovery. For example, clinical depression, which is common in many recovering alcoholics, as well as many recovering family members, sometimes has a biochemical origin. The feelings of sadness and emotional paralysis that are a part of this syndrome may not lift until a course of antidepressant medication is begun. In fact, this kind of medication may be necessary for a recovering individual to find the energy to begin pursuing activities and relationships that are important in stabilizing and maintaining sobriety. Alcoholics Anonymous publishes a helpful pamphlet concerning the use of psychoactive medications during recovery, entitled, *The AA Member—Medications & Other Drugs*. This pamphlet is generally available at meetings of Alcoholics Anonymous.

Q: Do you support the use of interventions to help move addicted people into treatment?

A: Intervention, which is described in Appendix I, is a powerful and positive method for helping alcoholics, as well as other chemically dependent people, accept the need for professional care. An addictions specialist should be able to help you determine whether an intervention is indicated for someone in your family, and she should be able to conduct it herself or refer you to someone who can.

It is unlikely that you will have the time or the inclination to ask all of these questions during your first meeting with a therapist. The consultation is often a difficult encounter for both patient and therapist. You might feel too tense or too embarrassed to say much at all. On the other hand, you may feel an urgent need to relieve yourself of the burden of fear, anger, and sadness you have carried for so long and find yourself using all fifty minutes of your session to pour out your story and your grief. However you use this time, you should feel that the therapist accepts your way of beginning the therapeutic relationship, and that she is making some effort to place you at ease. If, by the end of the first hour, you have not had the opportunity to ask all the questions you want to ask, you should feel free to ask for an extended consultation. That is, you should request that your relationship with the therapist remain tentative until you have time to ask your questions and develop some feeling of confidence that you are in the right place.

Sometimes, patients feel hesitant or shy about asking professionals to describe their professional beliefs and their approach to treatment. They are afraid of seeming intrusive or presumptuous. But protecting yourself and the interests of your family is one of the most important goals of recovery for people who have been caught up in self-destructive and self-neglectful patterns of behavior. Professionals who truly understand the psychological impact of addiction know that the ability to ask these sorts of questions reflects an inner strength and a determination to get better.

It is a good idea to steer clear of therapists who respond defensively to your requests for information. You should also give a wide berth to anyone who seems confused when you ask questions about intervention, family treatment, psychoactive medication, or the Anonymous programs. People who provide treatment to alcoholics and their families talk about these matters all the time, and have some point of view about them. A professional who doesn't have something to say about these components of recovery probably doesn't do much addictions work.

Finally, I would be leery of therapists who insist that there is one, and only one, path to recovery. An addictions specialist should have a basic philosophy that guides her work. I also believe that one tenet of that philosophy should be that sobriety is the only reasonable basis for recovery and *always* remains the chief priority of the patient and the treatment provider. A therapist must be prepared to take a tough stance about this issue at certain points in treatment. However, as previously noted, different people become addicted to the same drugs for different reasons, and different families have different responses to the same disease. Each alcoholic, and each family, has to work at devising a program of recovery that is most responsive to its unique set of conflicts and problems. When they make the decision that professional assistance is warranted, they have to find a therapist who is willing to devise this program with them.

Some therapists espouse a very rigid philosophy of recovery. They insist that every patient attend AA, or they assert that AA is not generally helpful. They demand a regimen of individual psychotherapy for every patient or they reject the idea of one-to-one treatment and prescribe group therapy for every patient. They declare that every family must be treated together, or proclaim that all family members should be treated in isolation from one another.

I find these unitary and stereotyped approaches to recovery destructive and disrespectful in their disregard for individual differences. I am far more comfortable with therapists who know and hold to the bottom line (sobriety), but are otherwise willing to experiment, willing to be surprised, and capable of responding creatively to a surprising situation. Your sense that you have found a therapist who is capable of both firmness and flexibility is a key indication that you have found a therapist who is likely to be a "good fit" for you and your family.

Finding a "Good Fit" with a Psychotherapist

"Goodness of fit" with a therapist is an elusive concept, to be sure. However, it is often a major factor in the success of psychological treatment. Your dentist's personality, or that of your internist, may seem irrelevant to you, especially if you seldom require intense and extended medical care. However, successful psychotherapy almost always involves an intimate, somewhat lengthy emotional involvement with a therapist. Therefore, it is as important to assess your compatibility with a particular mental health professional as it is to assess her technical qualifications to treat you.

Psychotherapists differ along a number of different dimensions. For example, they vary greatly in the amount of emotional warmth they are able to provide, their willingness to disclose their own feelings and experiences, and their tendency to provide direct feedback and suggestions concerning the problems you bring to therapy. Because you are an individual, with your own special needs and unique preferences, I can't tell you exactly what will feel "right" to you in terms of a therapist's personal style. However, the same conditions that inspire healthy development in the family situation are most likely to promote change and growth in psychotherapy. Although the therapy relationship is not intended to be a parental one, a good therapist, like a good parent, should be emotionally honest, emotionally stable, and emotionally responsive.

The Psychotherapist's Honesty

A therapist who is truly committed to emotional honesty in the therapeutic relationship will be willing to explore all important aspects of your emotional experience, including any feelings that pertain to her. She will also acknowledge errors when she makes them, arrange for consultation and support from other professionals as necessary, and take a firm stance if you engage in any behavior that threatens your physical well-being, or that of someone else. Let's examine these points one by one.

Encouraging Emotional Openness and Exploration. It usually takes some time for patients to develop the kind of trust in a therapist that allows them to express their deepest, and most painful feelings. However, you should find that your therapist encourages you to examine feelings of anger, fear, sadness, grief, or despair when these come up in the work. If you mention suicidal feelings, or problems with sexual functioning, your therapist should certainly try to draw you out about these issues. If you feel that any problem you raise has been treated lightly, or that the therapist changed the subject before you could discuss something that was troubling you, you should tell her so and she should be willing to go over the material again.

An emotionally honest therapist will also encourage you to pursue disturbing emotions when they are directed at her. This is a most important point. If you feel angry or disappointed in your therapist, or hurt by her, she should be very interested in hearing about it and ask you to explain fully what is on your mind.

Some amount of conflict is inevitable in the therapy relationship, just as it is in any extended, emotionally intimate human partnership. And, just as in "real life," miscues and misunderstandings between patient and therapist are typically the result of inadvertent errors made by both parties. These kinds of conflicts between the patient and therapist are frequently the basis for significant progress in the work, because they so often duplicate the sorts of problems that arise in the patient's interactions with significant others at home and at work. One of the more mysterious, yet profoundly valuable aspects of psychotherapy, is the fact that patient and therapist can unconsciously re-create, *together* a patient's deepest conflicts.

It *feels* bad to be in conflict with your therapist, but the good news is that you are now in a setting in which conflict can be observed and analyzed, as well as felt. This means that there is an opportunity for constructive change. However, the therapist's willingness to examine the conflict deeply and thoroughly often determines whether or not a conflict with a patient results in emotional growth.

It is natural for a therapist, who is, after all, a human being, to feel tense or defensive when a patient is angry at her, and you may feel her tension and irritability for a brief period when you make a complaint. However, if she is so uncomfortable with the thought of erring that she cuts off discussion with a quick concession and a change of subject, or stubbornly insists that the problem belongs to you and you alone, no gains can be made.

An emotionally honest therapist will support your right to make a complaint and will thoroughly examine her own behavior for evidence of error. She will understand that as a recovering alcoholic or codependent, you must find the courage and strength to address conflict with those who are close to you. She will take responsibility for mistakes in her handling of your problems or any wrongful information she has provided to you. She will not blame you for everything that goes wrong in the therapy. She will understand that there is an interactive aspect to nearly every conflict that occurs in human relationships and try to analyze what has gone awry in the dynamic between you. A therapist who does not do these things is a therapist who cannot accept the possibility that she has made a mistake. In the end, she will not be able to help you accept or love your own flawed humanity, and this is one of the most important goals of recovery from addiction and codependence.

There will be times when you find that it is simply too difficult to talk to your therapist about certain issues and feelings. A sensitive therapist will agree to put some things "on the back burner" until your relationship with her matures to the point where you feel freer to discuss the deeper issues that are troubling you. However, when she does this, you should feel that she is acting out of genuine respect for your position and your need to protect yourself, rather than responding to her own discomfort about discussing certain problems. One way to assess this is to note whether she comes back to these issues from time to time without prompting from you, and asks whether you now feel ready to take them on.

Acknowledging Professional Limitations. Just as the emotionally honest therapist concedes her errors when they occur (as they inevitably must), she also recognizes and acknowledges the limits of her professional expertise. She should not expect herself to handle every problem that arises in a chemically dependent family. Nor should you hold her to this unreasonable standard. At some point in your therapy, a crisis may develop, and either you, your spouse, or one of your children may require specialized, adjunctive treatment by another professional.

For example, when one of my patients, who was facing surgery for the first time, revealed that she had a long-standing phobia of needles and of receiving shots, I referred her to a behavioral psychologist experienced in the treatment of phobic disorders. I certainly know that phobias are generally treated with systematic desensitization, and I was even supervised in the use of this procedure in graduate school. However, I have never had occasion to use desensitization in my professional practice, and, after sixteen years, my skills in this area are rusty at best. Anyway, it is not my responsibility to be able to treat any problem a patient brings to me. It is my responsibility to know or to find out where to get just about anything treated and treated well. My phobic patient had approximately ten sessions with my colleague, and her problem was effectively resolved.

It will feel burdensome and stressful if your therapist asks you to have a consultation with another professional. It can be hard to develop trust and an open relationship with more than one therapist, but it is not healthy for you to remain isolated with your problems, and it is not healthy for a therapist to work in isolation from other professionals when she is treating complex problems like addiction and codependence.

Getting Tough. There are times when emotional honesty requires a willingness on the part of a therapist to face squarely the fact that a patient is behaving in a way that endangers herself or other people. It is the responsibility of a mental health professional to preserve your physical well-being when it is threatened, and to ensure that you do not bring harm to others. For example, if you are stockpiling pills and talking about the possibility of suicide, or if you are driving your children in the car when you have been drinking heavily, your therapist must face these issues directly and firmly. She must take some action even if you feel unable to do so. A therapist has the responsibility to insist on a psychiatric consultation, a hospitalization, or an intervention by a department of social services when your behavior presents a danger to yourself or others. She must also warn others if you have threatened to hurt them.

The Therapist's Stability

The emotional stability of a psychotherapist is reflected in the way she manages the boundaries of the therapy relationship.

The formal boundaries of psychotherapy involve matters of time, money, and privacy. It goes without saying that your therapist should generally be available at the time she has set aside for you, and that she should observe whatever arrangement the two of you have negotiated about a fee for her services. (Most therapists give about one month's notice if they intend to raise the fee initially set for a patient.) It also goes without saying that a therapist should never reveal your confidences to another person unless you have consented, in writing, to a release of your records, or unless your behavior presents an imminent danger to yourself or to someone else.

However, there are also psychological, emotional, and physical boundaries that an ethical and emotionally stable therapist observes with patients. Patients in psychotherapy are usually under some kind of intense emotional pressure. This can render them vulnerable to exploitation and abuse. Some therapists, emotionally troubled themselves, take advantage of this vulnerability.

Psychotherapy should always be conducted for the benefit of the patient and the patient only. Your therapist's goal should be to hear your story and to help you resolve your problems. She should not discuss her personal problems with you, she should not borrow money from you, and she should never suggest or accede to your suggestion of sexual intimacies of any kind.

The Therapist's Responsiveness

The most effective way to promote change and growth in a child or an adult is to support that individual's self-esteem, her feeling of personal value.

Some patients feel that the relationship with their therapist is fundamentally a business arrangement. They assume that a therapist is more interested in solving problems (and collecting a fee) than knowing patients as people. They believe that interpretations and interventions are based on the therapist's knowledge of psychiatric syndromes, rather than any deep feeling or concern for the patient's personhood. These kinds of relationships between patients and therapists do exist. However, a therapist cannot enhance a patient's conviction of personal value unless she is able to look beyond that patient's illness and beyond preconceived formulas for recovery. She must be able to sense a patient's positive resources—her grit, her power, and her creativity. She must feel such a genuine respect for these strengths that she is inspired to work, and work hard, to release them. This is the basis of emotional responsiveness in a psychotherapist—an ability to care for and esteem the whole person.

Authentic concern for the experience and well-being of another person is hard to quantify. It may be easiest to consider first what emotional responsiveness is not.

Certainly, emotional responsiveness has nothing to do with criticism or other behaviors that diminish others. Whereas a therapist may challenge your assumptions concerning life and the motivations of other people, she should never be emotionally abusive toward you. She should not shame or blame you for the difficulties you are having. She should not withdraw from you emotionally or appear to lose interest if you experience difficulty in making changes or in meeting goals you have established in therapy. Human survival depends on the ability to establish and adhere to fixed patterns of behavior. Biochemical processes in the brain work to maintain patterned behavior. Your patterns, as self-defeating as they may feel and be at times were established to help you survive harsh and hazardous circumstances. They can be altered, but it is only natural that change will occur slowly. An emotionally responsive therapist will help you to appreciate the fact that recovery (and psychotherapy) takes time. She will help you to proceed by encouraging you to explore the internal and external barriers to change in your life.

In a more positive vein, you should sense your therapist's effort to enhance your feeling of personal value in her attempts to understand your story, to empathize with your emotional dilemmas, and to grasp your pain and search for its origins. It should also be evident in her ability to identify and describe to you your strengths and achievements as a person. And you should feel that she takes genuine pleasure in your personal triumphs.

Conclusion

Good help can be hard to find. However, it is well worth the time and effort it takes to find the therapist who is right for you and your family. It is important to keep the following points in mind when you are looking for a mental health professional to help you with an addiction or with problems involving codependence.

- The addictions specialist may come from any of a number of types of academic and professional backgrounds
- However, she should have specialized training in the diagnosis and treatment of addictive disorders and codependence.
- She should also have the ability to recognize and treat other emotional problems, including depression and anxiety.
- The addictions specialist should understand that every member of an alcoholic family has been affected by the alcoholic problem, and that every member needs information and support and perhaps psychotherapy as well. If the specialist cannot provide what every family member needs (and this is frequently the case), she should be able

to make referrals to individuals or agencies who offer the other services that are needed.
- The addictions specialist should be thoroughly familiar with the
psychological and educational benefits provided through the Anonymous programs and should encourage participation in these
groups.
- The addictions specialist should treat the whole person—not just an
illness. She should promote your understanding and appreciation
for your personal strengths, and your unique value as a human
being.

≡ APPENDIX 1 ≡

Intervention

The technique of intervention was pioneered by Vernon Johnson, of the Johnson Institute, a chemical dependency treatment program in Minneapolis, Minnesota. An intervention can be performed at any time during the drinking or drugging career of an addicted person. However, the most recent trend in addictions treatment is to identify and treat chemically dependent individuals before they "hit bottom." If the addict can acknowledge her illness and the importance of sobriety *before* she loses all of the things she holds most dear in life—family, friends, and career—she will have an important incentive to remain in treatment. Thus, her prospects for a stable, and lasting recovery will be vastly improved. Intervention is a highly effective means of moving an addicted person into treatment at an early point in the development of her disease.

The format of an intervention is relatively simple. A group of family members, friends, and, perhaps, colleagues of a chemically dependent individual come together to speak with her about their concern that she is using chemicals in such a way as to seriously endanger her health, her family, and her job. The task of the interveners is also fairly straightforward. They must describe specifically the destructive behaviors that have frightened, angered, or humiliated them.

Although the concept of intervention *is* straightforward and simple, effective execution is often a tricky matter. Alcoholics are well practiced at deflecting information that may further erode their flagging self-esteem. Therefore, interveners must find a way to remain loving and supportive, even as they convey the bad news that the addict is sinking, and sinking fast. It is an attitude of love and the commitment to stand by the addict as she works toward recovery that is most likely to pierce her denial. Successful interveners must speak from a deep and sincere wish to see the addict restored to a condition of wholeness and health.

Most interveners have little trouble in identifying instances of erratic and abusive behavior that upset them, but it is hard for some to present this data in a loving way. They have been hurt so badly, and for so long, that their anger overcomes them when they are face to face with the addict, and they end up hurling accusations and insults at her. The addict retreats into her old pattern of denial and counterassault and the scene becomes a frustrating and futile re-creation of all the miserable struggles about drinking and drugging that have gone before.

Addictions specialists can often provide valuable assistance to concerned persons who wish to perform an intervention. Once people make the decision to intervene, they wish to move as quickly as possible. However, practice at citing specific events and sharing feelings nonjudgmentally is important, even for interveners who are in a fairly calm and rational frame of mind. It is absolutely essential for potential participants who are themselves in enormous pain. The addictions professional will usually take three to five sessions to prepare the intervention team and can even conduct the intervention if the team decides that this is desirable.

One great advantage of preparation and practice sessions is that the addictions specialist can track problems that participants are having with the concept or method of intervention. Many times, some additional support and guidance allow these problems to be overcome. At some point, however, the specialist may suggest, and the team may decide, that some participants are really not ready or able to intervene effectively. The ability to foresee and forestall catastrophic malfunctions of the intervention team is critical. Intervention is a major step and a powerful tool when it is performed well. You will want to give it your best shot. Therefore, it is best not to skimp on the practice sessions or the amount and quality of professional support you receive.

Interventions do not always result in the addict's immediate agreement to enter treatment. However, it often happens that even when an intervention "fails" in this regard, it constitutes an important first step in overcoming an alcoholic's denial. It is easy to fight off one, or even two people who say they love you and that they believe you are killing yourself. It is quite another matter to reject the concern of four, five, or six close people who sincerely believe that they are fighting for your life.

For a complete description of the technique of intervention, see Vernon Johnson's text, *Intervention: How to Help Someone Who Doesn't Want Help*. The full citation for this reference is given in the Suggested Reading section.

Suggested Reading

On Alcoholism, Other addictions, and Recovery

Johnson, V. E. *Everything You Need to Know About Chemical Dependence.* Minneapolis: Johnson Institute, 1990.

Johnson, V. E. *Intervention:* How to Help Someone Who Doesn't Want Help. Minneapolis: Johnson Institute, 1986.

Johnson, V. E. *I'll Quit Tomorrow.* New York: Harper & Row, 1980.

Robertson, N. *Getting Better: Inside Alcoholics Anonymous.* New York: William Morrow and Co, 1988.

On Codependence

Beattie, M. *Codependent No More.* New York: Harper/Hazelden, 1987.

Cottman-Becnel, B. *The Co-Dependent Parent.* Los Angeles: Lowell House, 1990.

Mastrich, J., and B. Birnes. *The ACOA's Guide to Raising Healthy Children.* New York: Collier Books, 1988.

Perrin, T. W. *I Am an Adult Who Grew up in an Alcoholic Family.* New York: Continuum Publishing, 1991.

Schaef, A. *Co-Dependence: Misunderstood-Mistreated.* New York: Harper & Row, New York, 1986.

Wegscheider, S. *Another Chance: Hope and Health for the Alcoholic Family.* Palo Alto, California: Science and Behavior Books, 1981.

Whitfield, C. *Healing the Child Within.* Deerfield Beach, Florida: Health Communications, 1987.

On Family Issues and Parenting

Ames, L. B., and F. L. Ilg. *Gesell Institute of Human Development Series.* New York: Dell Publishing, 1979.
(A series of books that describes the features of normal development in children of different ages. The books are entitled *Your One Year Old, Your Two Year Old,* and so forth, through age fourteen.)

Bettelheim, B. *A Good-Enough Parent.* New York: Vintage Books, 1988.

Faber, A., and E. Mazlish. *How to Talk So Kids Will Listen, and Listen So Kids Will Talk*. New York: Avon Books, 1980.

Fraiberg, S. *The Magic Years: Understanding and Handling the Problems of Early Childhood*. New York: Charles Scribner's Sons, 1959.

Francke, L. *Growing Up Divorced*. New York: Linden Press, 1983.

Greenspan, S., and N. T. Greenspan. *The Essential Partnership: How Parents and Children Can Meet the Emotional Challenges of Infancy and Childhood*. New York: Viking, 1989.

Greenspan, S., and G. H. Pollock, eds. *The Course of Life:* Vols. I, II, and III. Madison, Connecticut: International Universities Press, 1991.

Leach, P. *Your Baby and Child: From Birth to Age 5*. New York: Knopf, 1985.

Lovejoy, F. H., and D. Estridge, eds. *The New Child Health Encyclopedia*. New York: Delacorte Press, 1987.

Rubin, J., and C. Rubin. *When Families Fight: How to Handle Conflict with Those You Love*. New York: William Morrow and Co., 1989.

For Recovering Children

Black, Claudia. *My Dad Loves Me, My Dad Has a Disease*. Denver: M.A.C., 1974.

Hall, L., and L. Cohn. *Dear Kids of Alcoholics*. Carlsbad, California: Gurze Books, 1988.

Seixas, J. *Living with a Parent Who Drinks Too Much*. New York: Greenwillow Books, 1979.

For Adult Survivors of Sexual Abuse

Bass, E., and L. Davis. *The Courage to Heal: A Guide for Women Survivors of Child Sexual Abuse*. New York: HarperCollins, 1988.

Davis, L. *The Courage to Heal Workbook: For Men and Women Survivors of Child Sexual Abuse*. New York: HarperCollins, 1990.

Ratner, Ellen. *The Other Side of the Family: A Workbook About Abuse, Incest and Neglect*. Deerfield Beach, Florida: Health Communications, 1990.

Index